FOLLOWING JESUS

FOLLOWING JESUS

More about Young Children
and Worship

Sonja M. Stewart

Geneva Press
Louisville, Kentucky

Book design by Sharon Adams
Illustrations by David Hartman Designs, Inc.
Cover design by Pam Poll
Cover art: GREAT CATCH © 1993 by John August Swanson
Serigraph 22⅛″ x 31¾″

Represented by the Bergsma Gallery, Grand Rapids, Michigan, (616) 458-1776. John August Swanson paintings and limited-edition serigraphs are available from this gallery.

Full-color posters and cards of Mr. Swanson's work are available from the National Association for Hispanic Elderly. Proceeds benefit its programs of employment and housing for low-income seniors. For information, contact National Association for Hispanic Elderly, 234 East Colorado Blvd., Suite 300, Pasadena, CA 91101, (626) 564-1988.

First edition
Published by Geneva Press
Louisville, Kentucky

This book is printed on acid-free paper that meets the American National Standards Institute Z39.48 standard. ∞

PRINTED IN THE UNITED STATES OF AMERICA

00 01 02 03 04 05 06 07 08 09 — 10 9 8 7 6 5 4 3 2 1

Library of Congress Cataloging-in-Publication Data
Stewart, Sonja M., 1937–
    Following Jesus: more about young children and worship / Sonja M. Stewart.—1st ed.
        p.   cm.
    ISBN 0-664-50123-0 (alk. paper)
    1. Worship (Religious education) I. Title.
BV1522.S73 2000
268′.432—dc21   99-054945

To my parents

Rachel Olive Forgrave 1908–1999

and Malcolm Charles Forgrave

and

to my sons

Calvin, Todd, and Keith Stewart

Contents

ACKNOWLEDGMENTS ix

INTRODUCTION 1

Worship 8
Biblical Stories and Storytellers 21
Jesus and the Kingdom of God 28
Framework for the Story Presentations 35
Worship Center Order 49

PRESENTATIONS 55

God's Gift of Jesus the Christ

1. Baby Jesus Is Presented to God 57

Jesus Shows the Way of the Kingdom of God in Galilee

2. Follow Me 61
3. A New Teaching 65
4. Jesus and the Paralytic 69
5. Jesus and the Tax Collectors 74
6. Jesus Calls the Twelve Disciples 78
7. The Parable of the Farmer and the Growing Seed 82
8. The Parable of the Treasure 86
9. The Parable of the Fishnet 89
10. Jesus and the Storm 92
11. Jesus Heals Two "Daughters" 95
12. Jesus Feeds Five Thousand People 99
13. The Transfiguration of Jesus 103
14. Jesus Heals a Boy 107
15. Who Is the Greatest? 111

Jesus Shows the Way of the Kingdom of God in Jerusalem

16. Jesus Makes Lazarus Alive Again 114
17. The Parable of the Two Sons 118
18. The Most Important Commandment 122
19. The Gift of the Poor Widow 125
20. A Woman Anoints Jesus for Burial 128
21. Too Afraid to Follow Jesus 131

22. Jesus' Trial   135
23. Jesus Dies and God Makes Jesus Alive Again   139
24. Jesus Appears to Mary Magdalene   143
25. Jesus Appears to Thomas   147

*Jesus' Disciples Show the Way of the Kingdom of God
in Jerusalem, Judea, Samaria, and the World*

26. Jesus Commissions the Disciples   150
27. Jesus Appears to the Disciples by the Sea   154
28. Jesus Again Asks Peter to Follow Him   158
29. God's Gift of the Holy Spirit   162
30. Peter, Follower of Jesus, Heals a Lame Man in Jerusalem   167
31. Philip, Follower of Jesus, Teaches in Samaria   170
32. Dorcas, Follower of Jesus, Helps the Poor in Judea   175
33. John, Follower of Jesus, Teaches throughout the World   179
34. A New Heaven, a New Earth, and a New Jerusalem   183

APPENDIXES   187

Appendix A: Telling Stories over Fifty-two Weeks   189
Appendix B: Covering a Parable Box with Gold Paper   191
Appendix C: Materials for Following Jesus   192
Appendix D: Instructions for Making Parable Materials   202

PATTERNS   205

Acknowledgments

This book was made possible through the contributions of many people who have assisted in innumerable ways. I am grateful to Dean and Louis Griffith for a grant from the Griffith Foundation, which enabled me to begin the research and writing of this book, and for their personal interest and encouragement through the years. My thanks to Ben Johnson, who introduced me to the Griffiths and provided opportunities for me to present "Children and Worship Workshops."

I am indebted to many students, workshop participants, and children's worship leaders whose insights and accounts of children's responses helped to refine the stories and material. Special thanks goes to Tawnya Helmling, the mother of three of my grandchildren, who assisted me for ten years in leading workshops and even longer in telling these stories to children and keeping track of their responses.

Deb Abbott, Kay Beven, and Ginny Witte tested the stories in their worship centers, recording children's reactions and collecting some of their art responses. They also helped with designing some of the materials.

Sibyl Towner and Carolyn Rappenberger are faithful friends who have read my manuscript, provided feedback, and encouraged me during the years of writing this book. Sibyl introduced me to Patricia Garcia Garza of Monterrey, Mexico, who not only tested these stories with children in Mexico, El Salvador, and Spain but composed and recorded songs to accompany the stories.

Eleanor Vander Linde, a therapist for children and adults, listened to my concerns of how to present the passion narratives and wondering questions to young children. Kevin Otrhalik gets credit for the line "when they received the Holy Spirit, they were filled with so much love, . . . " which I have used in the last five stories.

Several friends made materials for me. Rachelle Oppenhuizen created the exquisite materials for "The Parable of the Farmer and the Growing Seed" and "God's Gift of the Holy Spirit." Carole Ardsma designed some patterns, such as the fish, the basket, and the border of the field. Carole Kendrick made the two mountains. Olivia Stewart designed the tomb.

Many others have encouraged me in numerous ways. Among them are Lynnette Colmey, Annette Schneider, Cynthia Sketters, Sharon Stewart, and Leonard Vander Linde.

I am grateful to my colleagues at Western Theological Seminary, to President Dennis Voskil and James Brownson, Dean for Academic Affairs, for their support of this project. Special thanks goes to Sally Vis and Beth Smith for their outstanding administrative support in helping to prepare the manuscript and the computer disks needed in the publication process and for their amazing ability to administer the annual "Children and Worship International Workshops."

INTRODUCTION

Introduction

In 1985 I changed. I began to reexamine what I had been taught about the religious formation of young children and in turn what I was teaching seminary students about children's spirituality. I have taught young children in inner-city public schools. I have also taught many Sunday school classes, founded two cooperative nursery schools, and been a director of children's ministries in a local congregation. I was applying in the church what I learned from public school education without ever questioning if the difference between school and church might argue for different environments and methods.

The church educational material I was using did not question this either. Church school classrooms mirrored those of the public schools, particularly those for teaching social studies. Biblical stories were used to teach theological concepts *about* God and Jesus. In other words, stories were used as illustrations for teaching a particular theological belief or moral. It seemed that there was little, if any, sense of the presence of God in the church school, for all it seemed we were doing was learning *about* God.

Moreover, I was taught that young children could not really know God. They were to grow up on their parents' faith. When they reached adolescence they were to decide for themselves who Jesus is and whether they wanted to follow him. I began to question this, asking, What if the young child can know God now, not just learn about God? What if young children do have a loving relationship with God?

Those questions led to the question that changed my approach to the Christian formation of children three through eight years of age. What, I asked, would happen if biblical narratives are told as stories in a *worshiping* environment that is specifically designed for young children? This is a three-pronged question that addresses (1) the design and order for a worship environment, (2) the content of stories told in that environment, and (3) how the stories are to be told. I set about designing and testing a worship environment, a sensorimotor story telling method and a particular way of constructing biblical story content, for young children.

I found that young children *do* have a fundamental awareness of the holy. Although they may not be interested in the various forms of religion prescribed for them, they *are* interested in God, and their faith can be formed as they are invited into the stories and parables of scripture. I also found that children bring their own lived experiences into the biblical stories, such as when, having told the story of Jesus feeding five thousand people, I watched a six-year-old boy draw a large circle on his paper. Next a smaller circle began to take the form of a hamburger, or perhaps a fish sandwich, and then french fries and a Coke appeared. To my amazement he drew a large M (those golden arches) and printed "Five Thousand Feed." Biblical stories, personal experiences, and the Holy Spirit interact so that children come to their own knowing of God, not simply an acceptance of information based on the authority of others. Children can have their own faith in God as children.

This book intends to show a way of being in worship with children five through eight years of age, although some of the stories may be appropriate for three- and four-year-old children. (If you design age-appropriate worship content and wondering questions, you can use the stories and parables with any age). Children love stories. When you tell biblical stories using the narrative language of scripture without embellishing the stories with extraneous details or turning them into lessons, children enter biblical stories with wonder, awe, and amazement. This is the way the people around Jesus responded when he told a story or performed a healing as he showed them the way of the reign of God.

Yet something more happens with Jesus' stories. God is revealed through them. Since God's self is revealed through the scripture, people are invited into a loving *relationship* with God. It is this relationship that draws both children and adults into worshiping God.

Young children require a sensorimotor worship environment to understand how to participate in the corporate worship of God. Young children learn first through their bodies, emotions, and senses. As you will see, children's worship centers are intentionally designed multisensory environments. Since God is revealed through biblical stories and parables, in the children's worship centers biblical stories and parables are "translated" into felt and wooden materials so the stories can be sensed, felt emotionally, and "read" visually as well as heard. The materials are constructed for the children's use, so the materials "live" on low, open shelves where they can be seen by and are accessible to the children.

Each story has its own tray, baskets, and materials necessary for telling the story. For example, each story has its own felt underlay and its own wooden figures. This allows the children to have access to all the materials for a story without having to hunt for or borrow from another story.

Each parable has its own gold parable box in which the materials for telling the parable are kept. Parable figures are not made of wood but usually of laminated material or felt.

When a story is told, the leader moves wooden figures on an underlay to represent the action in the story. Following the story, a group response time gives the children an opportunity for wondering together about the story. Next a personal response time invites children to use the story materials to retell, wonder, and work with the story, or to choose to work with other stories they have heard. Working with the biblical story materials gives children opportunity to wonder, and to try out hunches. To ask, "I wonder . . . ," "What if . . . ";

to move materials, see, feel, sense, smell, and form their images of the story; and to play their way into transforming insights. Many children use a variety of art materials to create their personal responses.

In this multisensory worship environment, personal and communal transformation may result through listening to the scripture, just as people were changed by following Jesus. In *The Transforming Moment,* James Loder, a professor of developmental theory and transformation at Princeton Theological Seminary, has shown that there is a logic to transformation and that biblical narratives and parables are constructed using a logic for transformation. I believe the order of worship is also constructed with the logic of transformation, which makes a worship environment a most appropriate place for children to deepen their love for God as they listen to and work with the stories of God. So the key to this new way I have designed for children's spiritual formation is a *worship context* instead of a school environment.

One outcome of designing a worship approach to the Christian formation of young children was the publication of *Young Children and Worship* (1989, Westminster/John Knox Press), which I wrote with Jerome Berryman and which has remained a best-seller since its publication. It describes the worship approach, provides instructions for helping young children learn to get ready to listen to God, and includes story presentations and patterns for materials.

This approach to worship with young children is different from the usual ways of teaching about worship. It shows children how to worship God instead of just teaching about worship. Worship flows from our love of God and requires active participation. It is difficult to describe worship in a book because it is experiential. The storytelling method is also difficult to describe because it is visual, oral, and kinesthetic.

To help leaders with this new approach, I created in 1985 "Children and Worship International Workshops." These workshops take place in a model worship center and demonstrate an affective way for leading children in worship. Workshop participants are shown how to prepare themselves spiritually, how to set up the worship environment, and how to tell the stories. The participants are given the opportunity to practice presenting the stories and to explore more deeply the theory and theology of this worship approach. Four-day "Children and Worship International Workshops" are offered annually in June at Western Theological Seminary, in Holland, Michigan. While attending one of these workshops is the best way to learn this approach, you can also arrange for me to teach a workshop elsewhere. These are generally shorter workshops and are usually scheduled over a weekend.

I have taught "Children and Worship Workshops" throughout the world and am encouraged to find this approach to be ecumenical and cross-cultural. There are "Children and Worship" worship centers in Canada, Mexico, Central America, the Virgin Islands, Japan, Taiwan, India, South Africa, Zambia, Spain, Great Britian, and numerous other places.

Many of you have already participated in one of my workshops. I thank those of you who are enabling thousands of children, around the world, to know and love God through your leadership in the worship centers. I have also heard your request for more stories. So I have written this book, *Following Jesus,* as a sequel to *Young Children and Worship.*

Following Jesus is written to stand largely on its own. It has its own organization. It is more than a selection of interesting, new stories to be inserted into *Young Children and Worship. Following Jesus* intends to extend and deepen five- through eight-year-old children's understanding of Jesus and his teaching of the way of the reign of God as it prepares them for Christian discipleship. The environment for telling the stories and parables continues to be the context of worship within a multisensory worship center designed for children.

I use the Gospel of Mark, with some exceptions, to provide a framework and sequence for following Jesus' life. The sequence of the stories allows young children to know the course of Jesus' life before they have a well-developed sense of chronology. It also helps them see Jesus' life as a whole life, rather than as a variety of unrelated events or stories about Jesus. It is my intention here to provide a way for children to follow Jesus through biblical stories, which show

- who Jesus is
- what he is teaching about the kingdom of God
- why Jesus is calling people to follow him
- what he is sending them into the world to say and do.

These are the same questions the first followers of Jesus struggled to answer over the three years they followed, watched, and listened to Jesus.

The story presentations are arranged in four categories:

> God's Gift of Jesus the Christ
> Jesus Shows the Way of the Kingdom of God in Galilee
> Jesus Shows the Way of the Kingdom of God in Jerusalem
> Jesus' Disciples show the way of the Kingdom of God in Jeru-
> salem, Judea, Samaria, and the World

The first section begins with the story of the baby Jesus being presented to God at the Temple in Jerusalem. Children enjoy hearing about Jesus when he was a baby. But more importantly I want to begin with a story of the incarnation, of God coming to us in Jesus the Christ. Simeon's and Anna's recognition of the baby as the promised Christ provides the story for this foundational belief of Christians.

The next two sections establish the ministry of Jesus, the adult, in two geographical locations, Galilee and Jerusalem. Two underlays help create Jesus' neighborhoods, first, in Galilee and later in Jerusalem.

For the second section, a blue and green felt underlay representing the Sea of Galilee and the area around the village of Capernaum (the home of Peter, where Jesus lived) provides the setting in which Jesus asks people to follow him as he shows them the way of the kingdom of God. He does this by casting out unclean spirits, healing the sick, forgiving sins, enabling paralytics to walk, stilling storms at sea, and raising the dead.

In the third section we meet Jesus' friends in Jerusalem as well as many people who are opposed to him. A notched, sandstone felt underlay representing the walled city of Jerusalem provides the setting for Jesus' last two weeks of life and his death and resurrection. As Jesus shows the way of the reign of God at the Temple, his authority is challenged more fervently by religious leaders who are trying to find a way to have him put to death. Jesus' disciples struggle to understand who Jesus is. Many women disciples remain faithful followers throughout, especially Mary Magdalene, Mary the mother of James and Joses, and Salome.

The fourth section shows the risen Jesus with his disciples, again in Galilee. From the mountain where Jesus first called the twelve disciples, he now commissions and sends his disciples into the whole world to continue his work, which they do after Jesus' ascension and their receiving the Holy Spirit at Pentecost. It is recorded in Acts 1:8 that Jesus said to his disciples, "But you will receive power when the Holy Spirit has come upon you; and you will be my witnesses in Jerusalem, in all Judea and Samaria, and to the ends of the earth." I chose one story from each of these locations to show the disciples doing what Jesus commissioned and sent them out to do. More information about the stories in each section is provided in "Framework for the Story Presentations" on p. 35.

The stories in each section are presented in a way that indirectly helps children answer the questions that Christians have asked since Jesus first called people to follow him:

- Who is Jesus?
- Do I want to follow him?
- Do I want to receive and enter the kingdom of God?

Since the worship center atmosphere and environment are essential to presenting the stories and parables successfully, in chapter 1 I address the meaning of *worship space* and how it is used in both corporate worship and in the children's worship centers and then address the meaning and structure of the fourfold *order of worship* as it is used in corporate worship and in the children's worship centers.

Worship

A SPACE FOR WORSHIP

It is an unusually beautiful Michigan day, after a week of gloomy, dreary, gray days. The January sun is teasing the shadows, the evergreens are dancing with the wind, and traces of green emerge through the snow. I think, for just a moment, that this is holy. This earth can be a holy place, a special place to be with God.

This sunny January day is reminding me that before people worshiped in buildings, they worshiped outdoors, on mountains or wherever else they had an experience with God. They built altars and marked places with stones to remember the God who was revealed there. The place of the landing of Noah's ark was marked with an altar, as were places where Abram and Sarai heard the voice of God. After God gave the law on Mount Sinai, the people placed it in an ark so the priests could carry the law as it led them on their journey in the wilderness. When they were not traveling, the ark was kept in the tabernacle or tent for God, where the people gathered to worship and offer sacrifices to God. Eventually, when peace was established in Jerusalem, King Solomon built the Temple, a house for God, as the special place to worship and offer sacrifices to God. As the dwelling place of God the Temple was believed to be the center of the earth; its architectural design symbolized the Garden of Eden, and its furniture, the exodus.

While we know that God can be worshiped anywhere, we still set aside special gathering places to worship God. However, since the building of the tabernacle in the wilderness, our place of worship has had an architectural design.

The architecture of Christian churches symbolizes our beliefs about God and how God is to be worshiped. Space, furniture, symbols, art, and holy writings combine to attest to God's creation and providence and form a special place to be with God. Most churches are built around the Lord's table or altar, which symbolizes the death and resurrection of Jesus, the Christ. It is at this table that Christ feeds us. We approach this table through the waters of baptism, and so the baptismal font is often at the entrance of the sanctuary.

Today we can no longer take it for granted that people know the meaning of the worship space or understand the order of activity that occurs there. We need to help young children understand the meaning of worship space by arranging a special worship environment in which we can tell them the stories of God and help them experience the symbol system of worship.

A Worship Center for Children

A children's worship center is an intentionally designed multisensory environment where children may worship God and where multisensory methods of biblical storytelling provide a way for children to enjoy the wonder, mystery, and awe of God. In what follows, I describe the meaning of the children's worship center by showing first its relationship to the *environment* of Sunday corporate worship and, second, its relationship to the *order* of the service of worship.

CHURCH AND CHILDREN'S WORSHIP CENTERS: SPECIAL PLACES TO WORSHIP GOD

Today we usually gather to worship God in a building. This ordinary building, a church, becomes a special space, which we often call a sanctuary. It is a special place that is considered holy or sacred. As a sanctuary, it also represents a safe place. Traditionally, a sanctuary is a safe place where we are not to be harmed. God meets us in this safe place where we can be who we are without fear. It is a safe place even when the rest of our world may be very dangerous.

Children's Basic Need to Be Safe

I give attention to the church as sanctuary to emphasize that, like a sanctuary, the children's worship center is to be a safe place. Children are to be and feel safe in the worship center. This helps meet their basic need for security, which is necessary as they discover so many new things. They need a secure environment in which to explore, wonder, puzzle, and create. The worship center provides a safe environment through a careful arrangement of the space and furniture, which remains the same for each session, as does the order of worship for the children.

A Sacred Symbol System for Worship

The church building in which we worship is designed to help us worship God and to bring to remembrance God's acts of creation and providence. Each Sunday is a "little Easter," a day to celebrate the death and resurrection of Jesus the Christ. Traditionally, Christ's table or altar symbolizes this belief. The pews or chairs we sit in usually face the table or altar, which in most Christian churches continues to be the focal point in the worship environment.

The baptismal font reminds us of our entrance into the Christian life, and our new life in Christ. Through the waters of baptism we have been washed clean and new. A lectern or pulpit, from which the Bible is read, reminds us that God is made known to us through listening to God's word. Moreover, stories of the Bible are often displayed in stained glass, banners, and other works of art. Look at the architecture and furnishings of your church to see how they symbolize beliefs about God and how God is to be worshiped.

Incarnation, Baptism, Eucharist, and Children

The children's worship center does not have a baptismal font, the Lord's table or altar, a lectern, or a pulpit. Instead children sit on the floor in a single circle around a low central shelf on which are placed the story materials that represent the incarnation, baptism, and the Eucharist. Around the rest of the room, on open shelves, are the other biblical story and parable materials. (Please see the diagram on p. 11.)

The Central Shelf

The shelf where the materials for the incarnation, baptism, and the Eucharist are placed is called the focal or central shelf. At the center top of the focal shelf are the nativity figures: the baby Jesus representing the incarnation, Mary, Joseph, a donkey, a shepherd, a sheep, three magi, and a camel. These figures serve to tell the story of when God came to the whole world in the person of Jesus the Christ. We are called Christians because of this belief. A cloth representing the color of the season of the church year is placed under these figures and is changed when the season changes. (For more information see pages 143–146 in *Young Children and Worship*.)

The shelf immediately underneath holds the colored cloths for each season of the church year. These are used as the underlay for the nativity figures and as the covering for the prayer table so that they correspond with the colors of the seasons of the church year. The church year puzzle is on the bottom shelf. (For more information see pages 126–129 in *Young Children and Worship*.)

On the top shelf to the left and right as you face the nativity are two other symbols of Christ. They relate to the sacraments of baptism and the Eucharist or Lord's Supper. To the left is the Christ candle, a large white candle that symbolizes Christ the Light. It reminds us that Jesus said, "I am the light of the world." Children come to understand baptism through the Christ candle and other materials that show how those who love the Light become one with Christ the Light. A white underlay remains under the Christ candle to represent the color the church usually "wears" for baptism.

The shelf immediately underneath holds a tray with candles and candleholders for each person in the worship center, a container for matches, and a snuffer. On the bottom shelf is a tray that holds a small baptismal bowl, a small pitcher of water, and a basket with wooden figures representing the ages of the people your congregation baptizes: an adult, a youth, and an infant if your church baptizes infants. (For more information see pages 72–74 and 212–214 in *Young Children and Worship*. Note that I have changed the materials from an infant doll in a white gown to the wooden figures.)

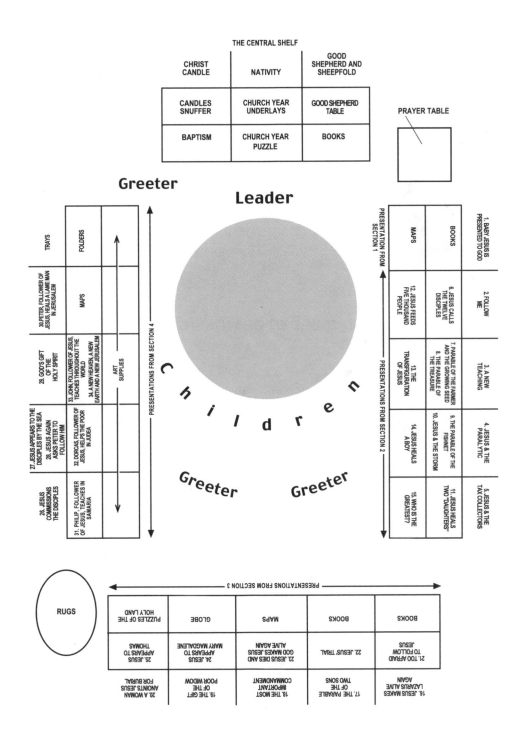

THE CENTRAL SHELF

CHRIST CANDLE	NATIVITY	GOOD SHEPHERD AND SHEEPFOLD
CANDLES SNUFFER	CHURCH YEAR UNDERLAYS	GOOD SHEPHERD TABLE
BAPTISM	CHURCH YEAR PUZZLE	BOOKS

PRAYER TABLE

Greeter

Leader

Children

Greeter   Greeter

TRAYS | FOLDERS

30. PETER, FOLLOWER OF JESUS, HEALS A LAME MAN IN JERUSALEM | MAPS

29. GOD'S GIFT OF THE HOLY SPIRIT | 33. JOHN, FOLLOWER OF JESUS, TEACHES THROUGHOUT THE WORLD | 34. A NEW HEAVEN, A NEW EARTH AND A NEW JERUSALEM | ART SUPPLIES

27. JESUS APPEARS TO THE DISCIPLES BY THE SEA | 28. JESUS AGAIN ASKS PETER TO FOLLOW HIM | 32. DORCAS, FOLLOWER OF JESUS, HELPS THE POOR IN JUDEA

26. JESUS COMMISSIONS THE DISCIPLES | 31. PHILIP, FOLLOWER OF JESUS, TEACHES IN SAMARIA

PRESENTATIONS FROM SECTION 4

PRESENTATION FROM SECTION 1

MAPS | BOOKS | 1. BABY JESUS IS PRESENTED TO GOD

12. JESUS FEEDS FIVE THOUSAND PEOPLE | 6. JESUS CALLS THE TWELVE DISCIPLES | 2. FOLLOW ME

13. THE TRANSFIGURATION OF JESUS | 7. PARABLE OF THE FARMER AND THE PARABLE OF THE GROWING SEED | 8. THE PARABLE OF THE TREASURE | 3. A NEW TEACHING

14. JESUS HEALS A BOY | 9. THE PARABLE OF THE FISHNET | 10. JESUS & THE STORM | 4. JESUS & THE PARALYTIC

15. WHO IS THE GREATEST? | 11. JESUS HEALS TWO "DAUGHTERS" | 5. JESUS & THE TAX COLLECTORS

PRESENTATIONS FROM SECTION 2

RUGS

PRESENTATIONS FROM SECTION 3

PUZZLES OF THE HOLY LAND	GLOBE	MAPS	BOOKS	BOOKS
25. JESUS APPEARS TO THOMAS	24. JESUS APPEARS TO MARY MAGDALENE	23. JESUS DIES AND GOD MAKES JESUS ALIVE AGAIN	22. JESUS' TRIAL	21. TOO AFRAID TO FOLLOW JESUS
20. A WOMAN ANOINTS JESUS FOR BURIAL	19. THE GIFT OF THE POOR WIDOW	18. THE MOST IMPORTANT COMMANDMENT	17. THE PARABLE OF THE TWO SONS	16. JESUS MAKES LAZARUS ALIVE AGAIN

On the top shelf to the right of the nativity are the Good Shepherd and a sheepfold with ten sheep. Underneath is the circle with the table of the Good Shepherd, a basket of five wooden adults and five children, and a small basket containing a beautiful miniature plate with bread and a chalice. Children understand the meaning of the Eucharist as they experience the Good Shepherd leading the sheep from the sheepfold to his table where he feeds them with special bread and a special cup. Next, as the sheep are exchanged for people, the children see that the Good Shepherd also feeds people at this table. On the bottom shelf are books about the sacraments. (For more information see pages 201–206 in *Young Children and Worship.*)

Shelves for Biblical Stories and Parables

To the sides of the central shelf are other open shelves, which hold the materials for the stories that are found in the "Presentations" section of this book. These New Testament stories are arranged to follow the sequence of Jesus' life and teachings of the kingdom of God. The biblical stories are told in a context of worship, which has an intentional order that directs the activity of worship.

THE ORDER OF WORSHIP

Children know, love, and can worship God. However, corporate worship is structured on and uses words and symbols based on stories and memories children do not yet have. For children to participate meaningfully in corporate worship, they need first to experience the essential parts and stories of worship through sensorimotor means. The children's worship centers are designed for this. They are also designed to create an environment that provides for children's need for security and repetition.

Young Children's Need for Security and Repetition

Young children feel safer when order and appropriate repetition are intentionally structured into the activity of the worship center. But children are not alone in this. Adults also have a need for the order of worship to remain the same each Sunday. In fact, when we worship with a congregation where the worship order is different from the order we are accustomed to, often our attention turns to the details: When do I stand up? When do I sit or kneel? How do I find my way around the book of worship or the hymnbook? It is very difficult to concentrate on worshiping God when the order of worship is unfamiliar.

In the children's worship center the same order is followed each session. This not only gives children a feeling of security and supports their need for repetition, but it also enables them to give attention to two things that *do* change—namely, the story or parable presentations and the responses. The fourfold order of congregational worship provides the framework for the flow of activity in the worship center.

THE FOURFOLD ORDER OF WORSHIP

In Christian worship, the scattered people of God gather to praise, listen, and respond to God by celebrating the creative and redemptive acts of God, particularly the resurrection of Christ. The order of the service helps us do this. Christian worship has a fourfold structure, regardless of denomination or tradition. Your service may be highly liturgical or informal, even spontaneous, but the fourfold order is there. This order reflects the ordinary social activities of family celebrations: gathering, listening and responding, thanking, and going. Expressed in the language of worship, this weekly celebration of the family of families uses particular terms to order the time together: "Assemble in God's Name," "Proclaim God's Word," "Give Thanks to God," and "Go in God's Name," for example.

Your church order may have different names for each part, but basically the functions are the same:

1. Assemble in God's Name (Gathering or Approach to God)
   We quiet ourselves and prepare to listen to God.
2. The Proclamation of the Word of God
   We listen and respond to God's Word.
3. The Thanksgiving (Eucharist)
   We celebrate the Eucharist by thanking God for God's many gifts of creation and providence, the gift of redemption in Christ, and the gift of the Holy Spirit. After this we receive the bread and the cup at the Lord's table.
4. Going in God's Name to Love and Serve the Lord (Sending)
   We are sent into the world in the power of the Holy Spirit to live as signs of the kingdom of God, living as Christ's ministers and missionaries.

THE ORDER OF WORSHIP AND YOUNG CHILDREN

In deciding what to use with young children from the congregational order of worship, I asked two questions: (1) What are the foundational and essential components of worship? (2) And what are the most essential biblical stories that give content and meaning to the images, symbols, and actions of worship? I examined each part of the order of worship, selected the most essential parts for young children, and designed a worship approach around these parts. What follows is a description of the four parts of the order of worship and what I chose from each part to do with young children.

1. Assemble in God's Name

The worship environment helps us come into the presence of God. As we gather, we try to become aware of the presence of God and get ready to listen to God. We do this by shifting from everyday time, space, and language to worship time and religious language. Although getting ready comes from within, the liturgy helps us refocus and center in God as it shifts our everyday language to religious or biblical language, images, symbols, and signs of God. What God has done for the world in the past is available to us through story and remembering. Time changes. It becomes slower. We do not have to hurry, and we can silence our noisy hearts so they can listen to God. The atmosphere, language, images, symbols, and signs of God invite us into a holy space where we can be with God. We greet one another in the name of the Lord. We sing and speak our praise to God. We confess our sins so that our relationship with God is restored and nothing stands in the way of our being with God. The order of worship as it is found in worship books is similar to this:

> Call to Worship
> The Greeting
> Hymn of Praise
> Confession and Pardon
> Response of Praise

Two things are essential in this first part of the order for worship: (1) our ability to get ready to be with God and (2) our awareness of the presence of God.

Gathering in the Children's Worship Center

In the children's worship center, the worship leader and greeters must arrive at least fifteen minutes before the children, in order to prepare themselves to be with God. The worship leader sits on the floor with her or his back to the central shelf (the shelf with the materials for the incarnation, baptism, and Eucharist), praying and preparing to listen to God. A worship leader who genuinely feels the presence of God models a way for the children to feel the presence of God. It is this prayerful preparation that helps the leader genuinely greet the children in God's name, enter the story as it is told, and be able to listen and respond to the children's wondering.

Greeters' prayerful preparation helps them calmly greet the children outside the door when they arrive. Here the children begin to prepare themselves to enter this special place to be with God. The children put things they've brought with them in "the safe place," where they won't be lost and the children can get them when they leave. If an offering is taken, the money is placed in a basket before the children enter the worship center. The basket is placed on the shelf below the shelf with the Nativity.

The leader greets each child as he or she sits on the floor on the circle. New children are introduced, and conversation continues until all are seated. Then the leader helps transform this time and place into a special time and place to be with God.

The Call to Worship

"This is a very special place," the worship leader says. "This is a special place because God is here. We have come to listen to God, to hear the stories of God, and to talk to God. When we're here we don't have to hurry anymore. We can walk more slowly, and we talk more softly because some people might be talking with God and we don't want to disturb them. This is a special place to be with God, to talk with God, to listen to God, and to hear the stories of God. So we need a way to get ready to be in such a special place with God. You can get ready all by yourself. You don't need me to tell you to get ready. Quietness comes from inside you, not from someone telling you to be quiet. Let's listen for the quiet."

The Greeting

"When we come together to listen to God," the leader says, "we greet each other in a way that is different from how we usually say hello. We exchange this greeting."

Leader: The Lord be with you.
Children: And also with you.

(At Easter use this greeting:

Leader: Christ is risen!
Children: Christ is risen indeed. Alleluia, alleluia!)

Songs of Praise

Then we sing songs of praise to God that help us quiet ourselves so we can listen to God. These are meditative songs, like "Be Still and Know That I Am God" or "Alleluia, Alleluia, Give Thanks to the Living God," which continue to help us get ready to listen to God as the biblical story or parable is told.

2. Proclaim God's Word

The second part of the order of worship is the Proclamation of the Word of God. God is known through the scripture. In a safe context, we engage in two actions during this part of the service:

> We *listen* to the scripture.
> We *respond* to it.

The order of congregational worship is like this:

> [Listening to the Word of God]
> Prayer for the Illumination of the Holy Spirit

Old Testament Lesson
Psalm
Epistle
New Testament Lesson
Sermon
[Responding to the Word of God]
Hymn, Canticle, Psalm
Creed or Affirmation of Faith
Baptism, Confirmation, or Commissioning
Prayers of the People

When we are ready to listen to God's word proclaimed through scripture and sermon, we want to receive it as God intends, so we ask the Holy Spirit to guide us as we listen and respond. God reveals God's self through the scripture. Since this is revelation, the intention is to engage in a relationship with God. We are invited into a way of knowing God that comes through entering and living in the scripture. This knowing includes "remembering," or *anamnesis.*

This kind of remembering is not the recalling of facts and concepts or information about God. Anamnesis is remembering a relationship that brings both the Christian communities' experience of God in the past and God's promised future into our present experience. When scripture is read, we enter it in a participatory way, thereby sharing the storyteller's experience of God. Furthermore, we bring our own selves and our lived experiences into dialogue with the biblical story or parable. The Holy Spirit is also present so that story, self, and the Holy Spirit meet in dialogue as we find ourselves being formed by God.

But just listening to God's word is not enough; the word of God invites response. We respond to the word in a variety of ways. Corporately we respond with a hymn, affirmation of faith, baptism, and prayers. Personally we may be responding in ways that invite transformation. We typically have one of two responses.

Sometimes when we hear the scripture read it confirms our lived experiences and our love for God. Responses of joy and love flow from our abiding in God. There is a sense of peace, joy, happiness, awe, and wonder as we abide in the presence of God.

Other times, when we hear a biblical story or parable, we experience dissonance, disorientation, or disruption as our personal lived experiences come into conflict with the scripture. We do not need to be afraid of or flee from this conflict, for conflict initiates transformation. It is a way the Holy Spirit engages us, inviting us to be healed or to change. By dwelling in the scripture and going through the conflict, the Holy Spirit enables the transformation. Sometimes this takes a long time, but God gives us all the time we need. For this reason the place of worship needs to be a safe place where dissonance can be engaged, struggled with, and gone through. It means unhurried time for wonder and for letting scripture's convicting power move us toward the transforming insight that reorients our lives and enables us to dwell in the presence of the Holy Spirit.

Listening and Responding to God in the Children's Worship Center

The actions of listening and responding to the word of God are the heart of worship in the children's center. A story is told and the children respond to it. Using a multisensory approach, the story is presented with wooden or felt materials children can work with individually after the story is presented and corporately responded to.

Listening to the Word of God in the Children's Worship Center. When the leader senses the children are ready to listen to the story, the leader goes to the shelf where the materials for the story "live," respectfully carries them to the circle, and places the materials on the floor. The leader says a prayer for illumination, asking the Holy Spirit to guide our listening and responses to the story. The words of Psalm 19:14 are often prayed: "Let the words of my mouth and the meditation of my heart be acceptable to you, O LORD, my rock and my redeemer." Or everyone sings Psalm 19:14, from "May the words of my mouth" (*Psalms of Patience, Protest and Praise,* by John L. Bell. Words and music © 1993 The Iona Community, GIA Publications, Chicago, 1993, p. 11.)

Next the leader places an underlay of felt or other material on the floor to provide a focal point for the presentation. Then the leader tells a biblical story to the children using wooden and felt materials, which are placed on the underlay to help the children visualize the story. The stories are told in biblical narrative form, using only the essential words, materials, and movements. The leader is not telling the story to entertain the children. Rather the leader wants to get out of the way so all may enter the story. The leader's eyes are focused on the materials during the storytelling because the materials are the vehicles into the story. Eye contact brings both leader and children out of the story, so eye contact is reserved for the response time.

Responding to God in the Children's Worship Center. The children respond to a story in two ways. First, there is a *group wondering time* when the children and leader wonder about the story together. This is a dialogical sharing of wonderings and experiences in the story, and a time to try out individual interpretations in a group context. Wondering together, in a group, encourages and helps the children clarify their thinking and interpretation.

Second, there is a time of *personal response* following the group wondering time. Each child has personal time to continue wondering or to choose how to respond to the story or the experience the child has had. The children can use both the story materials and the art materials at this time. Each child personally decides what "work" he or she will do. Since the orientation sessions have shown the children how to select a place to work and how to get their materials and put them away, the children freely move about the room "all by themselves." In this way they can interact with the materials as the Spirit moves them. (The orientation sessions are described in *Young Children and Worship,* "Getting Ready to be with God," pp. 55–70. To be successful in setting the

18   *Following Jesus*

atmosphere of the worship center, you must prepare the children by following these getting-ready sessions.)

Young children can express through art and movement what may be difficult for them to express with words. The story and art materials are the tools they use to respond to the story. Since this is their personal response time, no prescribed responses are prepared for them.

To give closure to the response time and to prepare for the third part of the order of worship, the children put their work away and return to the circle, where the story or parable of the day is read from the Bible. Because they have seen the story presented and personally worked with it, they can now mentally picture the story and bring memories to it as they hear it read, a skill they will carry into corporate worship.

3. Give Thanks to God (Eucharist)

The third part in the order of Christian worship is the Eucharist. The congregation basically follows this order:

> Offering
> Invitation to the Lord's Table
> Great Prayer of Thanksgiving
> The Lord's Prayer
> Words of Institution
> Breaking of the Bread, Pouring the Wine
> Communion of the People

At this solemn but joyful feast, we offer our thanksgiving to God through the Great Prayer of Thanksgiving (the Eucharistic Prayer). This is a Trinitarian prayer that gives thanks for the gifts of God, Christ, and the Holy Spirit. It has a threefold structure. First, we praise God for creation and providence, the covenant, the law, and the prophets. Then we join in the great acclamation of praise, "Holy, holy, holy Lord, God of power and might, heaven and earth are full of your glory. Hosanna in the highest. Blessed is the one who comes in the name of the Lord. Hosanna in the highest."

Second, God is praised for Jesus, the Christ—for his birth, life, death, resurrection, ascension, and promise of coming again. One of the responses of the people is this great affirmation of faith: "Christ has died, Christ is risen, Christ will come again."

The third part of the Great Prayer of Thanksgiving calls on the Holy Spirit to draw us into the presence of Christ, to make the breaking of the bread and the sharing of the cup a communion of the body and blood of Christ, that we may be nourished and be made one with the risen Christ. The congregation responds with "Amen," or with the Lord's Prayer and the Amen.

The breaking of the bread and the communion follow. The communion provides a way to address evil, suffering, and death and also to experience joy, hope, and life. The communion "remembers" through movement and action the mystery that death does not rule. Death is negated by Christ's resurrection. Life comes out of death. Here a beginning becomes an ending and that ending becomes a beginning. The broken body and shed blood of Christ provide meaning for the brokenness, violence, and destruction that occur daily. To the cup we bring our suffering, mingling it with the blood of Christ. Our suffering given to Christ becomes transformed, and we live as signs that resurrection life, not death, is the definitive reality. In the strength of this food we prepare to return to the world as signs of Christ's reign.

A "Feast" and Children

The Eucharist is not celebrated in the children's worship center. But indirect preparation for the Eucharist is. The atmosphere is one of joy, warmth, and fellowship. We offer prayers of thanksgiving, beginning responsively with the words of the entry into the Great Prayer of Thanksgiving.

> Leader: The Lord be with you.
> **Children: And also with you.**
> Leader: Lift up your hearts.
> **Children: We lift them up unto the Lord.**
> Leader: Let us give thanks to the Lord our God.
> **Children: It is right to give our thanks and praise.**

Then the children and the leader offer prayers of thanksgiving followed by a "feast," which replaces the traditional snack. We remember that every Sunday is a feast day celebrating the death and resurrection of Jesus the Christ. Each child prepares a "table" made by unfolding a white napkin and placing it on the floor in front of him or her. (The procedure is found in the section "Worship Center Order," pages 52–53.) Then the food for the "feast" is offered, such as fruit, cheese, bread, and water or juice. This is a pleasant time of talking and sharing, sometimes about great feasts that Jesus gave, like the feeding of the five thousand.

4. Go in God's Name to Love and Serve the Lord

Paralleling the first part of the service, which was a time for getting ready to listen and respond to God, the fourth part of the order of worship is a time for preparing to reenter the world as signs of the reign of God. The order typically follows these steps:

> Hymn
> Charge
> Blessing
> Benediction

We sing a hymn and are commissioned to be a source of God's healing in the world. We are then charged to go out into the world in peace, to render no one evil for evil, to love and serve the Lord. Finally, we receive the benediction, a good word, as a sign of God's presence with us through the Holy Spirit empowering us for ministry and mission. The benediction is a sign that we do not go out alone, in our own power. We go in the power of the Holy Spirit from whom we receive the courage, stamina, words, and gifts to be signs of God's reign in all times and places. Thus the dynamics of the flow of worship provide a way for weekly renewal as we "remember" the mystery of faith.

Sending the Children in Peace

As we prepare to leave the children's worship center, we sing until the parents arrive. A greeter tells each child when his or her parent comes. Then the child goes to the leader and receives a personal, affirming word, a benediction. A benediction is a good word about the personal worth and love that God has for each child. Speaking so no one else can hear, the leader whispers a very good word to the child, such as "The Good Shepherd knows your name and loves you." Or a fruit or gift of the Spirit seen in the child that day could be named, such as "Your joy helped me feel happy today. Thank you for your smile." Then add, "God goes with you. Go in peace." The intent is to ensure that each child truly goes in peace.

God, who is present in the sanctuary and the worship center, is not bound to these places. The experience of God and a vision of a safe place go with us, sometimes even into very dangerous places. The God who is with us in the worship center is with us in every time and every place. As God goes with us, we are able to go in peace to love and serve our God.

Signing

In the worship center, when we sing or engage in greetings and responses, we also use signing for the deaf instead of finger plays. Signing is another way we can talk to God and to each other. It is a concrete way to include deaf children in the activities, offer them the opportunity to participate, and teach others.

The language of signing communicates meaning, imagination, and memory just as words do. It portrays feeling and stirs emotion, and children value the experience of signing. As they learn to "read" the signs of songs, they also learn the gestures and movement used in telling the biblical stories and consequently the gestures the pastor or priest uses in worship, particularly in baptism and the Lord's Supper.

The following resources may be helpful: *The Joy of Signing* and *Talk to the Deaf,* by Lottie L. Riekehof; *Intermediate Sign Language,* by Louie J. Fant, Jr.; *Religious Signing,* by Elaine Costello, Lois Lehman (Illustrator); and *Signing: How to Speak with Your Hands,* Elaine Costello, Lois Lehman (Illustrator). For additional books on signing, visit Amazon's Web site at www.amazon.com and search for sign language.

Biblical Stories and Storytellers

When we read the Bible we are reading *ancient stories* that reveal the wonder and mystery of an amazing and wonderful God. As a child I was introduced to the Bible through stories that remained close to the biblical text. By the time I began teaching Sunday school, many biblical stories in the curriculum resources were full of description and definitions that were intended to help children understand the ancient Middle Eastern culture of the Bible. Although they were called stories, they sounded more like social science lessons that were written to help make the Bible relevant to North American culture. The room was arranged like a class in social studies. Sometimes children would be asked to *reenact* a story by dressing in costumes and pretending to be biblical "characters." Yet people of the Bible often remained distant "characters," from long ago and far away, and not members of our families. Worship was separated from study, and if it occurred at all, it was at the beginning or end of the time for education.

The new approach to children's spiritual formation that I am offering here and that is described fully in *Young Children and Worship* is a worship approach that views the Bible from a worship perspective. The stories presented here are written in a narrative form that intends to tell the most essential parts of a story. By keeping the story whole, that is, keeping it in its narrative structure, and keeping the parable as parable, we engage the world of the story or parable and experience the wonder and amazement it conveys.

To determine the content and write the story presentations for this book, I needed to understand the form and structure of biblical narrative and parables. I learned that biblical narratives are written with an economy of words so that only what is essential to the story is told. Any detail that is provided is important to the content of the story. The omission of definitions and unnecessary detail provides silences, time, and space through which the listener experiences the awe, wonder, and mystery of God who is revealed through the story.

This structure makes biblical stories interesting and meaningful for children. Young children have difficulty sorting out the essential from the extraneous, so they are helped when only the essential words are used in a story. This enables children to listen and remember the story better, and it gives room for their imagination and lived experiences to interact with the Holy Spirit. That in turn helps them deepen their understanding and love for God. If they want detail, they will ask for it.

The Synoptic Gospels open Jesus' ministry with his proclamation of the reign of God. Part of this proclamation takes the form of Jesus casting out unclean spirits, healing the sick, stilling storms, and raising the dead. These stories are sometimes called miracle stories. One purpose of these stories is to show that God and the rule of God are present in Jesus, who is the Christ, and that God has ultimate power. Both Matthew and Luke record that when John the Baptist was imprisoned, he sent two of his disciples to ask Jesus if he is the Messiah (Christ). Luke inserts before Jesus' answer, "Jesus had just then cured many people of diseases, plagues, and evil spirits, and had given sight to many who were blind" (Luke 7:21). Jesus answers John's disciples, "Go and tell John what you have seen and heard: the blind receive their sight, the lame walk, the lepers are cleansed, the deaf hear, the dead are raised, the poor have good news brought to them. And blessed is anyone who takes no offense at me" (Luke 7:22–23). John would have understood that Jesus was saying that he is the Messiah, because John would have recognized Jesus' answer as the signs of salvation quoted from Isaiah 29:18–19; 35:5–6; 61:1–3. Jesus' miracles are signs that the promised reign of God has come and is present in Jesus.

Biblical scholars show that the healing narratives follow a threefold pattern: a setting, the healing, and a witness to the healing. Within this pattern are other characteristics that intend to show that the focus of the story is on the healing itself and not on the person healed. The person is usually unnamed, the disease not described, and the response to the miracle is one of awe and amazement.

The story of Jesus' casting out the unclean spirit in Mark 1:16–34 can serve as an example. The setting or context is Jesus, in Capernaum, calling people to follow him. He leads them to the synagogue and begins teaching about the reign of God. His teaching astounds people because it is done with authority, unlike that of the scribes. Into this setting a man with an unclean spirit arrives. Note that the man is unnamed. We are told only that he has an unclean spirit, but there is no description of this spirit.

Next a conflict arises between the unclean spirit and Jesus. Just as Jesus' authority is being recognized by the crowd, it is being challenged by the crying out of the unclean spirit: "What have you to do with us, Jesus of Nazareth? Have you come to destroy us? I know who you are, the Holy One of God" (Mark 1:23–24). Note the power of the unclean spirit. It calls Jesus by name. It recognizes both who Jesus is and his divine stature, something others in the crowd do not know.

The healing, in this case, is when Jesus exorcises the unclean spirit with the words, "Be silent, and come out of him!" (Mark 1:25) The unclean spirit convulses the man, cries out in a loud voice, and leaves.

The witness to the healing usually comes from both the person healed and from those who saw it. The healed testify to being healed, and the others witness through their response of awe and amazement. In this case, there is no response from the healed person, who remains anonymous. However, the witness of the crowd is one of amazement. And they keep exclaiming, "What is this? A new teaching—with authority!" (Mark 1:27).

As you tell the miracle stories, you will notice that, in many, an unnamed person is healed. That focuses the attention on the healing or miracle itself and not on the person being healed. If any other detail is given about the miracle, such as when Jesus heals the woman who had been bleeding for twelve years or heals the boy after the transfiguration, that detail is given to help the healing stand out even more distinctly. After the healing or saving, as in the case of the disciples in the storm, there is a witness to the miracle, which is always one of awe and amazement.

In showing the way of the reign of God, some of Jesus' miracles show his power over nature. They connect us with (1) the story of creation, when God stilled the watery forces of chaos, and (2) words, by which God gave order to the cosmos. These miracles show that the power of God in creation continues through God's acts of providence. God's power continues to care for the created order, as the disciples see in Jesus' stilling of the storm on the Sea of Galilee. Their witness to this miracle follows that of other miracle stories: "And they were filled with great awe and said to one another, 'Who then is this, that even the wind and the sea obey him?' " (Mark 4:41).

Jesus also told parables to proclaim the reign of God. At one time the church thought of Jesus' parables as allegories. Later, biblical scholars believed parables to be illustrations with one main point. Current biblical scholarship holds that parables are extended metaphors, and so the meaning of a parable is contained within itself, as in a poem. So the parable should be stated whole. That is, we need to say the words of the parable, not reconstruct it into narrative or some other form of language.

Parables are two dimensional. They have an ordinary, everyday dimension and a metaphorical dimension. The reign of God enters the ordinary everyday life of real people—farmers, fishers, keepers of vineyards, and breadmakers. And it enters into real places—the Sea of Galilee, fields, vineyards, and homes. Into this ordinary world of human experience the reign of God enters and invites us to imagine another reality to which the ordinary points. Knowing comes by entering the parable and participating in the reality of the parable, not by standing outside and analyzing it.

To acknowledge the difference between narrative and parable, we use different materials for the presentations in the children's center. Materials for the narratives are made of wood. Materials for the parables are colored, mounted, laminated, and kept in gold boxes.

PREPARATION OF THE STORYTELLER

The worship leader's preparation as the storyteller is of utmost importance. The storyteller prepares by prayer and meditation until the story is formed in him or her. God's presence and a sense of God's greatness, mystery, and awe in the story need to become part of the storyteller. The storyteller's love for God and trust in the story, the Holy Spirit, and the children help form an atmosphere of expectation and freedom that permits interaction among God, the story, and the children.

Attending a "Children and Worship Workshop" gives the most complete training. If you cannot attend, then it will be helpful if you have someone already trained and experienced in this method present the story to you first. Read the story from the Bible and meditate on it. Then turn to the presentation section of this book, where the story and directions for moving the figures appear. After reading the presentation, reread the directions and try to visualize the movements you will have to make. Begin to practice the movements without saying the words aloud. Become familiar with the movement. You want to use no more movement than is necessary, so you need to know where to place the materials so they don't have to be moved unnecessarily. Sometimes you will need to start from the end of the story and move backward so that you can see the movement from beginning to end and how important the placing of materials is.

Move the wooden figures smoothly. Glide them; do not bounce or jump the figures when you move them. When you touch a figure, touch its shoulder, arm, or back. Place your hand near the feet or waist when moving it. Touching the top of the head and placing your hand on the face to move it is offensive. No one wants to be grabbed by the face or touched on the top of the head. Dragging figures by their faces treats them merely as figures instead of the people they are representing. In most stories you will move or trace the materials from your right to your left. This allows the children to see the movement in the same direction from which they read.

Parable figures remain flat on the underlay. When moving them, keep them on the underlay. Do not stand them up to move them. And again, place your hand on the figure's waist or back to move it. Do not move it by the face or push it by the head.

Next begin to learn the words, saying them aloud. It is important to say the words first and then move the materials, so the children first *hear* what happens and then *see* it. Since one part of the brain listens and another part sees, you enable the children to concentrate on the words without having to observe how the figures move at the same time.

You are not memorizing the story but internalizing it. As you practice, you want to begin to enter the story yourself. Keeping your eyes on the materials enables you to do this. Lifting your eyes will bring you out of the world of the story.

TELLING THE STORY

Arrive at the worship center at least fifteen minutes before the children. As you enter the room, let yourself begin to become centered in God. Check to see that the materials for the story are in order. Then sit on the floor with your back to the central shelf, which holds the materials for the incarnation, baptism, and Eucharist. Pray and ready yourself so when the children arrive, you feel the presence of God in you and also see the children as those in whom God is present. The Worship Center Order beginning on page 49 gives directions for helping the children get ready to listen and be with God. (Further instructions on how to help children get ready to listen are found in detail in *Young Children and Worship,* pp. 55–76.) When everyone is ready, walk slowly to the shelf to get the materials and carry them respectfully back to your place.

As you tell the story, you want to get out of the way so both you and the children can enter the story. You are not trying to entertain them. Your ability to enter the story will bring them into it. Several things you do will help. Pausing for a prayer of illumination helps give silence and a sense of the presence of the Holy Spirit. Smoothing the underlay helps you feel the story and provides a focal point for the children. You are beginning to transform the underlay into more than felt material. You remember the story through your hands as well as your mind. Your eyes remain on the underlay and make no eye contact until you begin the wondering questions. If you lift your eyes, it brings both you and the children out of the world of the story. Eye contact causes you to relate to each other instead of relating to God in the story.

As you tell the story or parable, say the words first. Speak meditatively and slowly because the sound and rhythm of your words are important with auditory thinking. Use only the essential words. Then move the materials without speaking. Do not be afraid of silence. It is providing a way to further interact with the story.

WONDERING TOGETHER

Group reflection and then a time for personal response follow the story. The group reflection is a time for wondering together. Wondering keeps the story or parable open to new interpretation and encourages dialogue with others.

The storyteller uses wondering questions to enable reflection and allow the children to share their feelings, experiences, and understandings of the story. Wondering together is a community's way of remaining open to the Holy Spirit, a way of meditating so the story becomes a part of the group's life. Wondering shapes and deepens our knowledge of God and what God desires of us. This knowing grows out of the children's experience of God, not from their being told what to believe about God. Their experience of God in the story informs their expression, and their expression, refined by the group, begins to name their world. This activity is the foundation on which theological thinking is built. Wondering together produces thinking Christians who can share their experiences of God and together discover God's calling for them.

Wondering questions are provided for you at the end of each story or parable. Choose several you would like to ask, but do not ask all of them. Since the wondering time is a dialogue between you, the children, and God, listen with empathy to the children. Respond in ways that keep the conversation open and allow the children to continue working with their feelings. (See *Young Children and Worship,* pp. 30–33, for more detail about the response time.)

TIME FOR PERSONAL RESPONSE

Personal response time follows the group time for wondering. It is not a time for free play. Each child chooses what he or she would like to do in response to the biblical stories he or she has heard. Working with story materials gives children opportunity for repeating the story or bringing their own lived experiences to the story. They use the materials for wondering and trying out hunches, as they work with the materials.

The children may choose to use art materials to retell a story or express their response to it. Art responses enable the children to express feelings and work through critical issues they cannot or do not wish to express verbally. Sometimes they resolve personal problems through their art, or the artwork may be a means of talking with God. Many responses show joy and happiness.

Since this time is intended to allow children to respond personally to the story, the leaders do not prepare art projects for the group. The children have the freedom to work on their own, using age-appropriate materials. Leaders do not entertain or interrupt the children's work by conversing with them. Instead leaders are a resource, and the children go to them when they wish help. If the material is being misused, however, the leader or greeter approaches the child and helps the child remember how it should be used.

Art responses take a variety of forms. Some have no apparent connection with the story. Some reproduce the story, while others are an interpretation of it. Some children work on existential issues in their drawings. The artwork functions like a personal journal, not a product to hang on the wall or refrigerator. The leader does not ask a child to explain what he or she drew. However a child may want to tell the worship leader about his or her work. The leader listens and responds with empathy rather than instruction. The children may take their work home or leave it in their special folders, which are available to them in the center. When compiled over several weeks, their artwork can be a spiritual journal that provides a way for the children to remember and build on their experiences in the stories.

RESPONSIBILITIES OF THE GREETERS

Greeters are extremely important to the atmosphere and functioning of the worship center. They are trained to understand how and why the worship centers function. Greeters are responsible for preparing the feast and developing a system for giving each child a turn to help in the center.

The greeters meet the children at the door and help them with their name tags if the children are not known by name. They help children put things they have brought with them in a special place so they do not get lost and can be picked up when they leave.

When new children come, greeters learn their names and briefly tell the children and their parents what happens in the worship center. Then a greeter walks with the child to the circle and introduces him or her to the worship leader and other children.

The greeters care for children who do not wish to be in the group. They may sit beside a child outside the group until the story is told and the child feels ready to enter the circle. If a child is disruptive during the story, the greeter gently touches him or her on an arm or gently touches with a circular motion on the back. Rarely does a greeter need to remove a child. Greeters function out of a centered quietness, so each child feels the love and security of the caring person even if the child is out of control.

During the personal response time, greeters help children carry heavy material, put on paint shirts, and do whatever they cannot do themselves. Greeters do not entertain or interrupt the children's personal time with the story unless a child's behavior is inappropriate.

Greeters choose children to help serve the feast. Children distribute napkins and food to the group, but greeters serve the water or juice.

The greeters meet parents at the door and tell each child who has come for him or her. After the children are gone, the greeters help straighten the room and make a list of supplies needed for the next session.

Jesus and the Kingdom of God

Children often learn the stories of Jesus as separate or disconnected stories and do not have a framework within which to organize them. The organization of the children's worship center environment and the sequencing of the stories of Jesus in *Following Jesus* provide a framework for organizing the stories of Jesus so that young children can perceive a sequential pattern in Jesus' life and teachings before they have a well-developed sense of chronology. By providing a structure for the stories, I hope that the children will see more than a gathering of isolated stories about Jesus. With a few exceptions, the order of the presentations follows that of the Gospel of Mark. The stories in Mark invite children to discover who Jesus is, why he is calling people to follow him, what he is teaching about the way of the kingdom of God, and what he is sending them into the world to say and do.

Mark's presentation of Jesus is particularly interesting to children, for in giving attention to people's feelings, Mark's stories show the awe, wonder, and mystery that surrounded Jesus. Mark's use of irony tells the reader from the start who Jesus is, even while the people around Jesus do not know. "Who is this man?" they ask. "Who is this man that unclean spirits listen to him?" "Who is this man that even the wind and the sea do what he says?" "Where does this man get his authority?" "Do I want to follow him?" "Do I want to show others the way of the kingdom of God?"

The stories are framed in two essential geographical locations: Galilee and Jerusalem. To help the children become familiar with what happens at these locations, I use a blue and green felt underlay to represent the Sea of Galilee and the land, and a sandstone, "notched" felt underlay to represent the walled city of Jerusalem.

Most of Jesus' teaching takes place in Galilee, around the village of Capernaum, where Jesus lives with Peter's family. It is here that Jesus begins to ask people to follow him. As they follow Jesus, they experience the way of the kingdom of God through both his actions and his teachings. It is here that Jesus casts out unclean spirits, heals the sick, and gives sight to the blind. Two essential questions are continually being asked about Jesus: "Who is this man?" and "Where does he get his authority?"

Jerusalem, on the other hand, is the place of the Temple. The Temple symbolizes the dwelling place of God and the center of the world. People go up to the Temple to worship and to offer sacrifices to God. In the time of Jesus every man who was able was required to go to the Temple to offer sacrifices during three feasts: the feast of Passover, the feast of Pentecost, and the feast of Booths. It is in the context of the feast of Passover that Jesus' death and resurrection occur, and in the context of the feast of Pentecost that the Holy Spirit is given to Jesus' disciples. It is in the Temple that the baby Jesus, as a firstborn male, is presented to God and recognized as the promised Christ. Simeon and Anna receive the baby Jesus, as the Christ, with great joy, but thirty-three years later, in this city, Jesus will be condemned to death for claiming to be the Christ.

There are three significant words and one phrase in the Gospel of Mark that I want to call to your attention. They are "follow," "immediately," and "authority." The phrase is "the kingdom of God." The word "follow" is used more than twenty times in the sixteen chapters of Mark. Jesus calls people "to follow" him, and they follow "immediately." Once we become aware of the word "follow," we notice that people are either being called to follow or they are following Jesus. We cannot ignore Jesus' call to follow him as an essential part of his mission. It is a call to be formed by Jesus and to join Jesus' ministry as one who will receive and enter the reign of God and in turn be sent to tell and show the way of the kingdom of God to others.

The word "immediately" is also commonly identified with the Gospel of Mark, where it is used about forty times. There is urgency in Mark to act "immediately." When Jesus calls Peter and Andrew to follow him, they immediately leave their nets and follow. The time is right, the time is now, and there is an urgency not to miss it.

A third word that calls for attention is "authority." The question, "Who is Jesus?" soon changes to "Why is Jesus doing this?" such as when the scribes wonder why Jesus eats with tax collectors. Behind the "why" question is really the question of authority. "Where does Jesus get his authority to say what he says and do what he does?" In Mark, the issue of authority emerges just after Jesus arrives in Capernaum. He begins saying to people, "Follow me." It is the Sabbath day and Jesus leads them to the synagogue, where he begins teaching. "They were astounded at his teaching, for he taught them as one having authority, and not as the scribes" (Mark 1:22). Later the scribes begin to question Jesus' authority, a questioning that continues until his last days in Jerusalem.

Mark's stories set up counterforces to Jesus' authority. Two forces are at work in Jesus' ministry—the authority of God as revealed through Jesus and the authority of other powers and principalities. There is the authority of Jesus and the authority of the scribes. There is the authority of Jesus and the power of "unclean spirits." There is the power of Jesus and the power of sin, as seen in the paralytic. There is the power of Jesus and the power of the cosmic chaos, as when Jesus confronts the storm at sea. And at Jesus' death, when it appears that the power of death is the ultimate authority, God raises Jesus from the dead. The ultimate authority is God, who has the power to overcome death and to give life.

Before I discuss the kingdom of God, I want to call to your attention to two events that precede Jesus' decision to proclaim the reign of God—Jesus' baptism and Jesus' temptation in the wilderness. These events are recorded in the Synoptic Gospels, that is, the Gospels according to Matthew, Mark, and Luke. They concern Jesus' decision to follow God in all he does.

WHO WILL JESUS FOLLOW?

In the Synoptic Gospels Jesus' public ministry is preceded by two important events: his baptism by John the Baptist and his temptation in the wilderness. These two stories record Jesus' call to follow the way of God throughout his ministry. First, Jesus receives the Holy Spirit at his baptism. When he comes out of the water, he sees the heavens open and the Spirit descends on him like a dove. He hears a voice from heaven saying, "You are my Son, the Beloved; with you I am well pleased" (Mark 1:11).

Then the Holy Spirit leads Jesus into the wilderness, where Jesus struggles with this call to proclaim the way of the kingdom of God. He must decide who he will listen to, who he will follow, and whose message he will proclaim. Satan, the tempter, is in the wilderness and puts Jesus to the test. Who will Jesus follow? Jesus' decision to follow God means he will proclaim the way of the kingdom or reign of God, which he does immediately when he returns to Galilee from the wilderness.

Biblical scholars agree that Jesus' central message is the kingdom, or reign, of God. Jesus never defines the reign of God, so it seems presumptuous to try to describe it. Yet it is an immense subject on which a great body of literature exists. Since the reign of God is the focus of Jesus' teaching and because it is of great significance in this book, I dare to reflect on some understandings of it.

The Synoptic Gospels—Matthew, Mark, and Luke—show that Jesus opens his ministry by proclaiming the kingdom of God. Mark, the earliest of the Gospels, tell us in the first chapter, "Now after John was arrested, Jesus came to Galilee, proclaiming the good news of God, and saying, 'The time is fulfilled, and the kingdom of God has come near; repent, and believe in the good news' " (Mark 1:14–15). The remainder of the Gospel of Mark shows the ways that Jesus announces the reign of God.

The Gospel of Matthew tells us: "Now when Jesus heard that John had been arrested, he withdrew to Galilee. He left Nazareth and made his home in Capernaum by the sea. . . . From that time Jesus began to proclaim, 'Repent, for the kingdom of heaven has come near' " (Matthew 4:12–13, 17). Then after calling Peter, Andrew, James, and John to follow him, verse 23 tells us, "Jesus went throughout Galilee, teaching in their synagogues and proclaiming the good news of the kingdom and curing every disease and every sickness among the people" (Matthew 4:23). From the beginning Jesus' proclamation of the kingdom is accompanied by casting out unclean spirits and other acts of healing. Proclamation and healing are joined.

Luke opens his account of Jesus' ministry with his teaching in the synagogues and provides an account of Jesus teaching on the Sabbath in the synagogue of his hometown of Nazareth. The kingdom of God is not mentioned, but characteristics of the nature of the reign of God are expressed in Jesus' reading from Isaiah 61. The words "good news" that appear in this reading are a synonym for "kingdom of God." Luke writes: "The Spirit of the Lord is upon me, because he has anointed me to bring good news to the poor. He has sent me to proclaim release to the captives and recovery of sight to the blind, to let the oppressed go free, to proclaim the year of the Lord's favor" (Luke 4:18–19). Instead of saying, "The kingdom of God is near," Jesus states, "Today this scripture has been fulfilled in your hearing" (Luke 4:21).

These three accounts from the Synoptic Gospels combine to give us five significant kinds of information about the reign of God.

1. They provide the basic terminology. Mark and Luke use the term "kingdom of God." Sometimes they use "gospel of God" or "good news of God," for in the Greek these words can also be translated "kingdom of God." Matthew uses the term "kingdom of heaven." These expressions are interchangeable and are equivalent in Greek manuscripts. Matthew may have preferred "the kingdom of heaven," because, as the most Jewish of the writers, he may have used it as a circumlocution for the divine name. (After 300 B.C. the Holy name, "God," was not to be said, so words like "heaven" were substituted, such as when the prodigal son says, "I have sinned against heaven," rather than saying, "I have sinned against God.")

2. They make the fundamental point that the kingdom of God means the reign of God. Its primary meaning is not realm, a static place, but the rule or reign of God, which is a dynamic, concrete, ongoing reality. It means the way of the reign of God.

3. They tell us the reign of God is a gift from God. For example, in Luke 12:32, Jesus says, "Do not be afraid, little flock, for it is your Father's good pleasure to give you the kingdom." The reign of God is a gift. The rule is God's, not ours. It is a reality that is not the result of human effort. If it were, it would be a human kingdom. We cannot build the kingdom of God. Jesus makes this clear when he teaches the disciples, "Let the little children come to me; do not stop them; for it is to such as these that the kingdom of God belongs. Truly I tell you, whoever does not receive the kingdom of God as a little child will never enter it" (Mark 10:14–15). We see from this statement that the kingdom is a gift that is to be *received* and *entered*. By receiving the kingdom of God we take it into ourselves. By entering we are going into it. Receiving and entering are a unitive act.

4. While Jesus proclaims the reign of God, he never defines it. It cannot be reduced to a definition. It is always more than can be articulated. People may not have understood Jesus' way of proclaiming the kingdom of God, but neither were they looking for a

definition. They were already familiar with the term, for it is used throughout the Old Testament. For example, Psalm 145 praises God as King and verses 10–13 say: "All your works shall give thanks to you, O Lord, and all your faithful shall bless you. They shall speak of the glory of your kingdom, and tell of your power, to make known to all people your mighty deeds, and the glorious splendor of your kingdom. Your kingdom is an everlasting kingdom, and your dominion endures throughout all generations."

5. In the New Testament a shift in verb tense indicates there is something new about the reign of God. In the Old Testament the future tense is used, such as, "It shall come to pass" or "On that day." Isaiah provides a messianic vision of when God's reign will be restored; on that day: "The wolf shall live with the lamb, the leopard shall lie down with the kid, the calf and the lion and the fatling together, and a little child shall lead them. . . . They will not hurt or destroy on all my holy mountain; for the earth will be full of the knowledge of the Lord as the waters cover the sea" (Isaiah 11:6, 9).

What is new in the New Testament is that the verb tense changes to the present. The kingdom *is* here. This *is* the gospel, the good news that the Synoptic writers told of in the opening of Jesus' ministry, "the kingdom of God has come near." Luke tells us clearly that, "Once Jesus was asked by the Pharisees when the kingdom of God was coming, and he answered, 'The kingdom of God is not coming with things that can be observed; nor will they say, 'Look, here it is!' or 'There it is!' For, in fact, the kingdom of God is among you" (Luke 17:20–21).

Yet while the reign of God is a present reality, it is also future, for its completion is yet to come. It is a reality that God is bringing about. We can say that the present reality of the reign of God comes to us from the past and yet out of the future. When the Gospels record that the kingdom of God is at hand, the imperfect verb is used, meaning that it is at hand but incomplete. It is happening and is continuing to happen. Its consummation will be in the future. That is why we continue to pray, "Your kingdom come. Your will be done, on earth as it is in heaven" (Matthew 6:10). As noted earlier, we receive and enter the reign of God. We receive it now, and in the future we shall receive the reign of God fully come. We enter the kingdom now, and in the future we shall live in its completion.

The passage from Luke 4 quoted earlier presents us with another characteristic of the kingdom, for it brings the person of Jesus and the kingdom of God together. The new understanding that Jesus brings is his identification of the reign of God with himself. This link between Jesus, gospel, and kingdom can be seen by comparing Mark 10:29, Matthew 19:29, and Luke 18:29. The context is the same for each: a wealthy man asks Jesus what he must do to inherit eternal life. Jesus loved him, and said, "You lack one thing; go, sell what you own, and give the money to the poor, and you will have treasure in heaven; then come, follow me" (Mark 10:21). The man left grieving, for he had many possessions. Then Peter mentions that they have left everything to follow Jesus.

The Synoptic Gospels all record that event, but each has Jesus speaking a different phrase to equate himself with the reign of God. Jesus says that there is no one who has left all and followed him "for my sake and for the sake of the gospel" (Mark) or "for my name's sake" (Matthew) or "for the sake of the kingdom of God" (Luke) "who will not get back very much more in this age, and in the age to come eternal life" (Luke 18:29–30). Here Jesus, gospel, and kingdom are linked and considered one and the same. To experience Jesus the Christ is to experience the reign of God. So the early church recognized that the new understanding Jesus brought was the identity of the kingdom with his self. Thus to proclaim Jesus as Messiah or Christ is to proclaim the kingdom of God.

The identification of the Messiah with the kingdom of God was foreign to rabbinic thought, for the ideas of the messiah and the reign of God were quite separate for Jews. The Jews, for many centuries, were ruled by foreign powers. In the time of Jesus, they were under Roman occupation. They longed for the day a messiah would come. For some, this meant that a messiah would overthrow all foreign powers, the kingdom of God would be established, and the messiah would become their king. Others were preparing for the imminent arrival of the kingdom of God, which would involve them in a war against the powers of darkness. All evil would be destroyed and paradise restored. Expecting a powerful military ruler, they were not prepared for a suffering messiah who would give his life for the salvation of people.

For Jesus, the kingdom of God was a gift for all peoples, not only for the Jews. This is seen in Jesus' ministry to the Gentiles, when in the country of the Gerasenes he casts out legions of unclean spirits from the man living among the tombs (Mark 5:1–20). And he cast out an unclean spirit from the daughter of the Gentile Syrophoenician woman (Mark 7:25–30).

Jesus' teaching of the reign of God is revealed in his very person—how he lives, speaks, and acts. If we want to know the way of the kingdom of God, then we look at who Jesus is and what he does, and we listen to what he says. He has authority over unclean spirits. He heals the sick, gives sight to the blind, and gives hearing and speech to the deaf. He feeds the hungry, converts sinners, and forgives sins. He demonstrates in his very being the kind of ruler God is. He embodies the kingdom of God.

Jesus teaches about the kingdom of God by telling parables. These parables are not illustrations about the reign of God but are extended metaphors. We must enter the parables to experience the mystery of the kingdom and to discover how we are being called to live as ethical citizens under the reign of God.

Jesus' call to receive and enter the kingdom of God is a call to conversion or transformation. It is a call to see reality from God's perspective rather than our own. Dwelling in the Holy Spirit, we receive the power to live the new commandment that Jesus gave us: "Love one another. Just as I have loved you" (John 13:34). Through the Holy Spirit we are given the power to do what Jesus did and said and to become signs of the reign of God.

To abide in the kingdom of God is to begin to experience what someday we will fully receive, as envisioned by John when he wrote: "See, the home of God is among mortals. He will dwell with them; they will be his peoples, and God himself will be with them; he will wipe every tear from their eyes. Death will be no more; mourning and crying and pain will be no more, for the first things have passed away" (Revelation 21:3–4).

John also envisions a new city of God and writes: "I saw no temple in the city, for its temple is the Lord God the Almighty and the Lamb. And the city has no need of sun or moon to shine on it, for the glory of God is its light, and the kings of the earth will bring their glory into it. Its gates will never be shut by day—and there will be no night there. People will bring into it the glory and the honor of the nations" (Revelation 21:22–26). With gratitude we receive and enter the reign of God now. And we wait in hope for the final consummation of God's reign.

To listen to the Gospel writers and especially to the Gospel of Mark is to contemplate these questions, which Christians for two millennia have addressed:

> Who is Jesus?
> What is the way of the kingdom of God that Jesus is proclaiming?
> Who gave Jesus authority to proclaim the way of the kingdom of God?
> Do I want to follow Jesus?

The children address these questions as they listen to the stories of Jesus engaging the people around him. Through wondering together and working with art and presentation materials, the children have the opportunity to work with these questions.

Framework for
the Story Presentations

One goal for this book is to provide worship leaders and educators with a framework in which children's love for Jesus will deepen as they hear of the unfolding of Jesus' life as a whole, rather than as unrelated stories about Jesus. The arrangement of the story presentations provides a way for children to follow Jesus through biblical stories that show who Jesus is, what he is teaching about the kingdom of God, why he is calling people to follow him, and what he is sending them into the world to say and do.

The presentations in this book are organized in four sections. The first section is entitled "God's Gift of Jesus the Christ," followed by "Jesus Shows the Way of the Kingdom of God in Galilee," "Jesus Shows the Way of the Kingdom of God in Jerusalem," and "Jesus' Disciples Show the Way of the Kingdom of God in Jerusalem, Judea, Samaria, and the World."

GOD'S GIFT OF JESUS THE CHRIST

Baby Jesus Is Presented to God

The children first meet Jesus as a baby in the story "Baby Jesus Is Presented to God." Jewish law required that every firstborn male be designated as holy to God. The Gospel of Luke tells of Jesus being taken to the Temple in Jerusalem to be presented to God and that God reveals to Simeon and Anna that this baby is the long-awaited Christ. Here is a story of the incarnation, of God coming to us as the Christ in a baby named Jesus. Note that the announcement that Jesus is the Christ occurs at the Temple. In a sense Jesus' life begins and ends at the Temple. And in a sense the Temple ends in the death and resurrection of Jesus the Christ.

When Simeon saw Jesus, he prayed to God, "Master, now you are dismissing your servant in peace, according to your word; for my eyes have seen your salvation, which you have prepared in the presence of all peoples, a light for revelation to the Gentiles and for glory to your people Israel" (Luke 2:29–32). Some churches still sing Simeon's prayer of thanksgiving, which is known as the Song of Simeon or *Nunc Dimittis.* It is sometimes used in evening prayer as a way to end the day and enter sleep in peace, for our eyes have seen our salvation in Christ.

I begin with this story because children enjoy hearing about Jesus as a baby. But more important, I want to begin with a story of the incarnation. This is no ordinary baby. This is the long-awaited Christ. This story can be told not only at Christmas but every day, because the incarnation is celebrated all year long and not just on Christmas Day.

Children's artwork, drawn after they hear this story, often portrays great joy. One picture showed Jesus being held up for the world to see, like Simba in *Lion King.* Another child drew Mary and Joseph in football jerseys with a large "M" on Mary's jersey and a "J" on Joseph's. Baby Jesus was being carried under Mary's arm like a football.

JESUS SHOWS THE WAY OF THE KINGDOM OF GOD IN GALILEE

Follow Me

This story takes place by the Sea of Galilee at the town of Capernaum, where Jesus will live with Peter's family. For three years Galilee is the primary location of Jesus' teaching. To help the children grasp this geographical location, a green and blue felt underlay is used to represent the land and the Sea of Galilee. To help draw the children into the story, the worship leader slowly traces the edge of the sea with a finger and says: "This is the Sea of Galilee. So many important things happen by the sea that we need a small piece of it to help us tell the stories. The sea is a wonderful and strange place. When the wind blows, the sea becomes very rough and wild. But when the wind is calm, the sea is very peaceful and still."

Then the leader introduces some of the people of the village to establish further the setting, or neighborhood, for Jesus' teaching of the kingdom of God. The worship leader says: "Many people live by the sea. Some are poor." Wooden figures are used to represent the people and are placed along the sea as they are identified. "Some are sick," the storyteller continues. "Some are children. Some are in the business of fishing." Peter and Andrew are named, placed by the sea, and shown casting their net into the sea. Then a boat is placed in the water and James and John, their father, and a servant are placed in the boat, where they are mending their nets. The scene is set. The worship leader sits back, pauses and begins the story. "Once there was someone who came to the Sea of Galilee. He said many amazing things and did such wonderful things that people began to follow him. He came close to the sick. He encouraged the poor. And he enjoyed the children. 'This is the way God wants us to care for each other,' he said. 'This is *the way of the kingdom of God.*' But they did not understand, so he said, 'Come. Follow me. I will show you the way. I will show you the way of the kingdom of God. Come. Follow me.' "

Because I want, first, to help the children hear Jesus' request to follow him, I end this story by showing the people following Jesus. This allows the children to wonder where Jesus might be leading them. We see in the next story that Jesus is leading them to the synagogue.

In this story I did not identify the person who came to Galilee as Jesus. Not only does this add mystery, but also it allows the unclean spirit, in the next story, to be the first to name Jesus and identify him as the Christ. However, each time I have told this story, the children have known that this person is Jesus. They seem to feel they have a secret that the people in the story aren't party to.

The first five stories in this section use a green and blue Galilean underlay, and in each the words quoted above are used to set the story in or near Capernaum. You will recognize that each story presents a different way in which Jesus shows the way of the kingdom of God. A separate underlay is needed for each story.

A New Teaching

"A New Teaching" is a continuation of "Follow Me" so it uses the same setting, underlay, and introductory words. It is the Sabbath, and Jesus leads the followers to the synagogue in Capernaum and begins to teach. A synagogue is a place for prayer and teaching. The people are astounded because Jesus teaches like a person with authority, unlike the scribes (teachers of the law). As quickly as Jesus' authority is recognized, so is it challenged by the power of an unclean spirit who, unlike the crowd, knows Jesus' name and who he is. The unclean spirit recognizes Jesus as the Christ. But Jesus is more powerful than the unclean spirit, and, by words, he casts out the unclean spirit. The people are amazed and wonder, "Who is this that even the unclean spirits do what he says?"

The scientific and medical knowledge with which we live is sometimes projected onto this story, and this makes it difficult to hear or tell the story. We don't want to talk about unclean spirits. We want to find a medical name for the condition of the man with the unclean spirit. But that is not the worldview of the people around Jesus. We are asked to enter the amazing world of this story to discern what is happening. How is it that an unclean spirit knows Jesus as the Christ, but the people do not recognize Jesus? This is not a medical story. This is a story of struggle for authority between the power of the Spirit of God and the power of another spirit. It is challenging, but we must enter this story and the amazing world it creates to come to an understanding of what it is like when God reigns.

Jesus and the Paralytic

Jesus is teaching in Peter's house, where a huge crowd has gathered. A paralytic is brought to Jesus. Seeing the paralytic, Jesus says, "Your sins are forgiven." By forgiving sin, Jesus does what, according to Jewish understanding, only God has the authority to do. Knowing that the scribes are questioning his authority, Jesus says to them, "But so that you may know that the Son of Man has authority on earth to forgive sins"—he said to the paralytic—"I say to you, stand up, take your mat and go to your home" (Mark 2:10–11). The man did, and everyone was amazed and glorified God.

As you are also amazed by these stories, begin to make note of the various ways Jesus is showing the way of the kingdom of God. Also, reflect personally on your image of Jesus as his identity emerges through these stories. Who is he?

Jesus and the Tax Collectors

Capernaum is a border town situated along the *Via Maris* (the way of the sea), a major trade route from Damascus to Egypt. The Romans, who were occupying Palestine, hired Jews to collect tolls or taxes from people wanting to use the road. Jewish tax collectors were considered traitors because they worked for the Roman government. Consequently, Jews were not to associate with them. Now as Jesus is walking along the shore, teaching about the kingdom of God, he sees Levi, a tax collector, at the tax booth. Jesus calls Levi to follow him and further violates Jewish religious and cultural values by eating with Levi and other tax collectors and sinners in Levi's home. Levi (Matthew) changes and becomes not only a follower of Jesus but also one of Jesus' twelve disciples.

Jesus Calls the Twelve Disciples

Since Jesus' arrival in Capernaum, crowds of people have followed him. Through his person, his teachings, and his actions, they are experiencing the way of the kingdom of God. With awe and wonder, they witness Jesus teaching with authority, casting out unclean spirits, forgiving sins, healing many people, and converting tax collectors and sinners. Now Jesus calls twelve of them to follow him in a special way. He calls and sends the twelve disciples throughout the villages to do what he has shown them: to tell of the way of the kingdom of God, heal the sick, and cast out unclean spirits.

The Parable of the Farmer and the Growing Seed

Again Jesus is teaching by the sea. The crowds have become so large that, to keep from being crushed, Jesus teaches from a boat. He is teaching in parables. Parables are extended metaphors. They have a concrete, everyday, earthly meaning that points to other meanings. From the boat, Jesus looks out upon fields that produce barley, wheat, and other foods. Perhaps it is planting time or harvest when he tells this parable. No matter, the crowd is familiar with farming. Jesus tells them the parable of the sower. Later, to a smaller group, perhaps again at Peter's house, he tells two parables about the kingdom of God. One is the parable of the farmer and the growing seed. This parable has often been referred to as "the seed growing secretly," but the attention is really on the farmer who knows the exact time of the harvest and gathers it.

The other parable Jesus tells in this series is the mustard seed. Only the parable of the farmer and the growing seed is presented in this book. The other two can be found in *Young Children and Worship* (pp. 156–58 and 166–68).

The wooden figures used in the worship center for the stories change to felt and colorful laminated materials for the parables. The parable materials are kept in gold parable boxes. This change reflects the change in the type of religious language being used. The metaphoric language of parables is different from the language of story or narrative. In *Young Children and Worship* I suggest grouping the parable materials on a parable shelf. In this book I suggest placing the parable materials with the story materials because the sequence and the geographic location from which Jesus told them are significant for understanding them.

Wrap the parable boxes in plain, gold foil paper to look like presents and to show that parables are very precious, like gold (directions are given in Appendix B). Parables are gifts, which have been given to us, so we can't steal or buy them. They have lids, so they are hard to enter, but when we do, we find something very precious.

Each parable has its own felt underlay. The materials are not made from wood as they are for the stories. Parable materials are colored, mounted, and laminated (directions are given in Appendix C). They are placed and moved flat on the underlay. Do not stand the parable figures when moving them as you do the wooden figures in the stories.

The introductory words for the parable box are at the beginning of this parable. If the children are unfamiliar with this introduction, repeat it when telling the other parables in this book.

The Parable of the Treasure

The parable of the treasure is found in the Gospel of Matthew. "The kingdom of heaven is like treasure hidden in a field, which someone found and hid; then in his joy he goes and sells all that he has and buys that field" (13:44). The parable does not tell us how the treasure was found. And that is not important to the parable. In a day without banks, and particularly in times of war, people hid their valuables, as was the case with the Dead Sea Scrolls, which were discovered in caves at Qumran. Palestine is a land of many rocks and caves. I have chosen to have the treasure found in a rocky area bordering a field. This parable is followed by the one about the merchant in search of fine pearls; on finding one pearl of great value, he went and sold all that he had and bought it. These parables convey the ultimate joy one finds in entering the kingdom of God. There is no greater value. This parable should be told with joy. I have used the phrase kingdom of God instead of kingdom of heaven because I have found that some children associate kingdom of heaven only with the place people go when they die.

The Parable of the Fishnet

In Matthew the parable of the fishnet is told immediately after the parable of the treasure and the parable of the pearl. These latter two parables show the joy of the people who desire to receive and enter the kingdom of God. But taken as a whole, Jesus' parables have a variety of perspectives about the kingdom of God. The perspective in the parable of the fishnet differs from that of the above parables. In this parable the kingdom of God is like a net thrown into the sea which catches fish of every kind; when it was full they pulled it ashore, sat down, and put the good fish into baskets but threw out the bad. Children identify with the good fish and are delighted when good is separated from evil. Adults sometimes find this parable troubling and often it fills them with tension. Do not be afraid of this tension. Dissonance initiates transformation for those who stay with the conflict and move through it. Parables call you to make ethical decisions. Play with the parable until an insight comes to show you what ethical decision God is calling you to make.

Jesus and the Storm

After an interval of teaching in parables, Jesus' authority is set in opposition to the power of the chaos of the cosmos. The power of cosmic chaos is represented by the windstorm on the Sea of Galilee. One is reminded of the story of creation, when "the earth was a formless void and darkness covered the face of the deep, while a wind from God swept over the face of the waters" (Genesis 1:2). Just as in creation, chaos is stilled by the word of God, so Jesus' words to the wind and the sea—"Peace! Be still!"—brought a dead calm. The disciples were filled with awe and wonder. Again the question of Jesus' identity is raised: "Who then is this, that even the wind and the sea obey him?" (Mark 4:41). The underlay is entirely blue to focus on the sea and to imply a danger. Be sure to use a boat that is deep enough so the disciples do not fall out when you toss it about in the storm.

Jesus Heals Two "Daughters"

In this story Jesus heals two unnamed women: the daughter of Jairus and a woman with a hemorrhage. The story of the healing of the woman who had been bleeding for twelve years is framed by the healing of Jairus's daughter, which means that it links with Jairus's daughter. The word "twelve" is a clue. The woman has been bleeding for twelve years. Jairus's daughter is twelve years old, the time for the beginning of menstruation. A bleeding woman was unclean and anyone who came in contact with her became unclean. Also anyone who touched a dead person was unclean. So in both cases Jesus becomes unclean. In showing the way of the kingdom of God, Jesus restores both women to life and calls one "daughter," saying, "Go in peace." Jesus has challenged the uncleanness laws, showing that the reign of God gives wholeness, life, and health.

Jesus Feeds Five Thousand People

The context of this story is the return of the disciples from proclaiming the kingdom of God throughout the villages. They are tired, and Jesus is taking them to a quiet place to rest. However, a great crowd follows them. The language used in this story reminds one of the words and actions of the Eucharist. Jesus *takes* the bread, *blesses* it, *breaks* it, and *gives* it to his disciples, and they give it to the crowd. The people continue to misunderstand who Jesus is and immediately want to make Jesus their king, so he slips away. This story takes place outside of Capernaum, on a hillside overlooking the Sea of Galilee. An all-green felt underlay is used to help the children connect this story with three others they may already know: "Jesus' Last Passover," "The Good Shepherd" parable, and "The Good Shepherd and the Lord's Supper," all found in *Young Children and Worship*.

The Transfiguration of Jesus

Toward the end of Jesus' Galilean ministry he takes his disciples to Caesarea Philippi, a beautiful village almost a thousand feet above sea level, at the foot of Mount Hermon. This is the farthest north that Jesus takes his disciples. Mount Hermon is the highest mountain to the north; Mount Sinai is the highest in the south.

Caesarea Philippi is a site of one of the main sources of the Jordan River. It was also a town of many religions, and it claimed to be the birthplace of the Greek god Pan. In this area, surrounded by the religions of the world, perhaps standing in view of many temples of Syrian and Greek gods, Jesus asks his disciples the question that so many have been asking about him: "Who do you say that I am?" Peter answers, "You are the Christ." Then Jesus tells them the first of three predictions of his coming death; he will go to Jerusalem, be killed, and on the third day God will raise him from the dead. This is so completely foreign to their concept of the Christ that they can not believe him. They expect him to become king and overthrow the Roman government. It is as if, after all the time they have been with Jesus, they are still blind to what he has been teaching them about the reign of God. In fact Mark emphasizes their blindness by framing Jesus' three predictions of his death and resurrection with two stories of the healing of blind men, the first at Bethsaida (Mark 8:22), and later Bartimaeus at Jericho (Mark 10:46–52).

Six days after Peter's confession that Jesus is the Christ (a clue to expect an epiphany), Jesus leads Peter, James, and John up a high mountain where the transfiguration occurs. This mountain is probably Mount Hermon, although Mount Tabor has been considered the traditional site. There is much symbolism in this story. They are on a high mountain. Mountains were considered holy and the place where God meets those on earth. Moses is associated with Mount Sinai and the giving of the law, while the prophet Elijah is associated with Mount Horeb and Mount Carmel. Elijah and Moses suddenly appear beside Jesus. They represent the prophets and the law.

Next a cloud representing the glory of God separates the three disciples from Jesus, Elijah, and Moses. A cloud both conceals and reveals God. When the glory of God settled on Mount Sinai, the cloud covered it for six days. A cloud led the way of the people through the wilderness, and a cloud had kept Moses from entering the tent of meeting. Now the cloud keeps the disciples from seeing Jesus, but they hear the voice of God, saying, "This is my Son, the Beloved; listen to him!" (Mark 9:7).

Jesus Heals a Boy

This story occurs as Jesus returns to his other disciples from the mountain where he was transfigured. The context is still the disciples' lack of understanding of who Jesus is and their inability to heal this boy. It is as if they were deaf to Jesus' teaching. Jesus heals the boy who cannot hear or speak, as the boy's father pleads with Jesus, "I believe; help my unbelief!" (Mark 9:24).

The course of Jesus' ministry shifts with his transfiguration. Now Jesus begins his last journey to Jerusalem.

Who Is the Greatest?

As Jesus and his disciples are returning to Capernaum on their way to Jerusalem, Jesus again tells his disciples that he will be killed and on the third day God will raise him from the dead. Their disbelief continues, and they argue over who is the greatest. When they arrive at Peter's house, Jesus asks them what they were arguing about on the way. Then he takes a child in his arms and instructs the disciples that "whoever wants to be first must be last of all and servant of all" (Mark 9:35).

Later, as Jesus continues to lead them on the way to Jerusalem, he tells his disciples a third time of his coming death and resurrection. Many are becoming afraid to travel with him.

I did not write additional stories about Jesus' teachings on the way to Jerusalem, so you might wish to tell the stories of "Jesus and the Children" and "Jesus and Bartimaeus" from *Young Children and Worship* (pp. 178–79 and 180–82). They help the children travel with Jesus on the way to Jerusalem. Both are from the Gospel of Mark. The story of the healing of blind Bartimaeus is the end frame for the three predictions of Jesus' death.

JESUS SHOWS THE WAY OF THE KINGDOM OF GOD IN JERUSALEM

Jesus Makes Lazarus Alive Again

This story takes place in Bethany prior to Jesus' arrival for Passover. Bethany is a village about two miles southeast of Jerusalem. When Jesus goes to Jerusalem, he stays with his friends Lazarus, Mary, and Martha. Lazarus is dying, and his sisters, Mary and Martha, send for Jesus. Jesus' disciples do not want him to go because people in Jerusalem want to stone him to death. Jesus delays going to Bethany, not because of the disciples' fear, but to wait until Lazarus is dead.

The Jewish tradition for preparing a body for burial was to wash it and then anoint it with sweet-smelling ointment. A cloth was placed over the head. The hands and feet were bandaged, and then a linen cloth with spices in it was wrapped around the body. The body was placed in a tomb that only family members could use and a stone was rolled across the entrance and marked to indicate a body was decaying there. Eventually the bones were placed in a box called an ossuary.

Since the wooden figure for Lazarus is not designed for bandaging the hands and legs, place only a small cloth over his head and wrap the rest of the body in a larger linen cloth.

Note that in this story, Martha is the one to identify Jesus as the Christ. Also note Jesus' authority over death as he raises Lazarus from the dead. Because of his action, many decide to follow Jesus, but the chief priests and Pharisees become more determined to find a way to put him to death. So Jesus retreats to the town of Ephraim, near the wilderness, where, according to John, Jesus remains until six days before the Passover.

Jesus then returns to the home of Lazarus, Mary, and Martha. The next day, he makes the triumphal entry into Jerusalem. You might want to tell the story of the triumphal entry, which is called "Jesus the King," from *Young Children and Worship* (pp. 186–88).

The next stories in this section take place in Jerusalem. Jesus' authority continues to be questioned by people who are looking for a way to have Jesus put to death.

To help the children make the transition to Jerusalem a sandstone felt underlay in an approximate shape of the city of Jerusalem is used to represent the site. Three sides of the underlay are notched to represent the walls of Jerusalem; for unlike the village of Capernaum, Jerusalem was a walled city. The side opposite the leader is not notched to convey the feeling of being in the city. To help the children imagine being in Jerusalem and to draw them into the story, the worship leader slowly traces the edges of the Jerusalem underlay with a finger and says, "This is the city of Jerusalem. So many important things happen in Jerusalem that we need a small piece of it to help us tell the stories." To set the context of Passover the leader continues with these words, "Once every year the people of God go up to Jerusalem to celebrate the feast of the Passover, to remember how God led them through the waters to freedom. And every year, Jesus and his family and friends go up to Jerusalem to celebrate the feast. But this year, . . . " Words specific to each parable or story follow.

The Jerusalem underlay changes in two of the passion stories. In "Too Afraid to Follow Jesus," the Jerusalem underlay changes from sandstone to navy blue felt and the Mount of Olives, made of hunter green felt, is attached to your left side of the Jerusalem underlay. The change in color represents the darkness of night.

In "Jesus Dies and God Makes Jesus Alive Again," the Jerusalem underlay is made from sandstone felt, but apple green felt is attached to your right side of the underlay to represent the place of Jesus' crucifixion and burial. You might want to look at a map of the city of Jerusalem and locate for the children the Temple area, the Mount of Olives, Bethany, the area for crucifixions, and the probable place of Jesus' burial.

The Parable of the Two Sons

Jesus is now in Jerusalem for Passover and is teaching at the Temple. This parable is framed by a conversation between Jesus and the chief priests and elders, who are questioning Jesus' authority. Jesus does not answer them directly. Instead he tells this parable that enables him to challenge the behavior of the chief priests and elders. If the children are unfamiliar with the introduction to a parable box, please use the introduction from the "Parable of the Farmer and the Growing Seed," on page 82.

The Most Important Commandment

Another challenge to Jesus' authority occurs at the Temple, where he is asked, "What is the greatest commandment?" This story is told on the Jerusalem underlay, and among the materials is a piece of red heart-shaped felt on which the words of the two great commandments will be placed. Each commandment is written on half of a white heart-shaped card, and the halves are placed together on the red heart. Perhaps the children will connect this with the story of "The Ten Best Ways to Live" from *Young Children and Worship* (pp. 108–11).

The Gift of the Poor Widow

The poor widow, who gives all that she has to the Temple treasury, in some respects brings to mind the parables of the pearl and the treasure as well as the disciples who leave what they have and follow Jesus. It is one thing to be willing to give one's whole life to follow the way of the reign of God. But does this woman know Jesus, and is she giving in response to her love of God? Or, as some scholars wonder, was she being taken advantage of by the religious authorities, who conditioned her to accept their values and support their religious institution at the cost of everything she had to live on?

A Woman Anoints Jesus for Burial

Jesus has left the Temple and is in Bethany visiting in the home of Simon the leper. While the disciples still deny Jesus' oncoming death, an unnamed woman disciple believes Jesus, enters the house, and anoints his head with expensive ointment. Anointing was done for two reasons: to honor a king and to prepare the body at death for burial. This woman's actions do both. She recognizes the kind of ruler Jesus is and anoints him as "king," and she anoints him in preparation for his death. The disciples scold her, but Jesus stops them and declares: "Truly I tell you, wherever the good news is proclaimed in the whole world, what she has done will be told in remembrance of her" (Mark 14:9). (Since this story occurs in Bethany, the Jerusalem underlay is not used.)

Too Afraid to Follow Jesus

The twelve disciples, who have been following Jesus for three years, are becoming too afraid to follow him. After Jesus' arrest, the disciples flee, except for Peter, who follows from a distance. But while listening to Jesus' trial from the courtyard, Peter is accused three times of being a follower of Jesus. Three times he denies it. At the crowing of a rooster, Peter realizes that he has betrayed Jesus. Striken with guilt and grief, he leaves, breaks down, and weeps.

The Jerusalem felt underlay is dark blue, which represents the darkness of the night of the arrest of Jesus. (Later you will see how several things in this story connect with the postresurrection appearance of Jesus to his disciples by the Sea of Galilee.)

Jesus' Trial

The repentance and death of Judas, one of Jesus' twelve disciples, occurs in the context of Jesus' trial. Judas received thirty silver coins to betray Jesus. As Judas sees that Jesus has been condemned to die, he realizes that he has betrayed an innocent person. Judas repents and goes to the chief priests and elders to return the money and to confess his sin. They are indifferent. Judas throws the money on the Temple floor and leaves. Overcome with guilt and despair, Judas commits suicide.

The story provides an opportunity for children to address appropriate and inappropriate ways to handle guilt and grief. The wondering questions provide ways to compare the way Judas handled his guilt and grief with the way Peter handled his in the previous story. This story takes place during the day in Jerusalem so the color of the Jerusalem underlay is sandstone.

Jesus Dies and God Makes Jesus Alive Again

The story of Jesus' death must always include the telling of his resurrection. While the wondering questions, in this story, give occasion to wonder about the crucifixion, they are followed by the announcement of Jesus' resurrection. It is imperative that you tell the children that God raised Jesus from the dead, after which you may continue more wondering. To hear that Jesus dies is difficult for children. Some of them cry. Be able to grieve with them, *and* be sure to tell them the wonderful news that Jesus is alive because God raised him from the dead.

No one was ever crucified or buried inside the city walls of Jerusalem. So the Jerusalem underlay is glued to green felt that represents the area of crucifixion and burial. People were buried in tombs hewn out of rock. Only family members could be buried in the same tomb. Joseph of Arimathea does an amazing thing when he places Jesus in his own tomb, in which no one has been buried.

Jesus Appears to Mary Magdalene

Each of the Gospels tells that Jesus' first postresurrection appearance was to Mary Magdalene. For those following the Common Lectionary, this story is told every Easter. Mary Magdalene is the first witness to Jesus' resurrection, but each Gospel reports variations of this account. In this story, after seeing Jesus, Mary Magdalene reminds the disciples to return to Galilee. Jesus is going there ahead of them, where they will see him, just as he promised. This sets the stage for telling the story of the great commission, which takes place on the mountain where Jesus called the twelve disciples.

Jesus Appears to Thomas

The second Sunday of Easter is traditionally called "Doubting Thomas Sunday." It gives those like Thomas a chance to discuss their doubts and to reflect on Jesus' conversation with Thomas. The risen Jesus appears to the disciples in a house with locked doors. Thomas had not been there, and he did not believe they had seen Jesus. For Thomas, seeing is believing. The next week Thomas is in the house and Jesus appears again. Jesus tells Thomas to look and touch the nail prints in his hands and to touch his side. Then Jesus says, "Blessed are those who have not seen and yet have come to believe" (John 20:29).

JESUS' DISCIPLES SHOW THE WAY
OF THE KINGDOM OF GOD IN
JERUSALEM, JUDEA, SAMARIA, AND THE WORLD

Jesus Commissions the Disciples

Jesus had instructed his disciples to return to Galilee, where he would meet them after his resurrection. They return to the mountain where the twelve disciples were first called to follow Jesus in a special way. From this same mountain, Jesus now sends them into the whole world to proclaim the reign of God. Jesus' words that send them are called the great commission: "All authority in heaven and on earth has been given to me. Go therefore and make disciples of all nations, baptizing them in the name of the Father and of the Son and of the Holy Spirit, and teaching them to obey everything I have commanded you. And remember, I am with you always, to the end of the age" (Matthew 28:18–20). These words are used in some liturgies for the sacrament of baptism when the person is presented for baptism.

The green and blue felt underlay for Galilee is used in this story, as is the mountain where Jesus first called and sent out his twelve disciples.

Jesus Appears to the
Disciples by the Sea

The story of the appearance of the risen Jesus by the Sea of Galilee is told in two parts in order to emphasize the resurrection of Jesus and then focus

on Jesus' conversation with Peter. Seven disciples are at Peter's house, perhaps grieving the absence of Jesus. Peter decides to go fishing and the others join him. The first part of this story allows the children to focus on the joy of
these seven disciples as they recognize Jesus and once again enjoy being
with him. Again the green and blue Galilean underlay is used, as are the boat
from the earlier stories and a charcoal fire, like the one in "Too Afraid to Follow
Jesus." The fish are made of wood.

Jesus Again Asks
Peter to Follow Him

The story "Jesus Appears to the Disciples by the Sea" is retold and then the
conversation between Jesus and Peter is added. This story and the passion
story, "Too Afraid to Follow Jesus," have several things in common. A charcoal
fire is used in both stories. The three denials of Peter are countered here with
Peter's three affirmations to Jesus' three questions: "Do you love me?" And
here at the place by the sea where Jesus first called Peter to follow him, Jesus
once again says to Peter, "Follow me!"

God's Gift of the Holy Spirit

It was not until the disciples received the Holy Spirit at the feast of Pentecost
that they were empowered to do what Jesus had commissioned them to do.
The disciples could not and were not to act on their own power. As Jesus'
authority and power were from God, so the disciples received their authority
and power from God through receiving the Holy Spirit. Only then did their fear
leave them and they began to be signs of the reign of God to the whole world.

The story "Pentecost" is in *Young Children and Worship* (pp. 209–11). This
story tells of the seven gifts of the Spirit that are named in Isaiah 11:2–3a. One
of the symbols of the Holy Spirit is the seven-tongued flame, which reminds us
of these seven gifts of the Holy Spirit. In the baptismal liturgy of many
churches, after the baptism with water, the minister lays hands on the head of
each person baptized and prays: "O Lord, uphold [the name of the person] by
your Holy Spirit. Give *him / her* the spirit of wisdom and understanding, the
spirit of counsel and might, the spirit of knowledge and the fear of the Lord,
the spirit of joy in your presence, both now and forever." The underlay for this
presentation is a red seven-tongued flame onto which alternating yellow and
orange "tongues of fire" are placed as the seven gifts of the Spirit are named.

Jerusalem, Samaria, Judea,
and the Nations

Just before the ascension of Jesus and ten days before Pentecost, Jesus
appears to his disciples and says, "You will receive power when the Holy Spirit
has come upon you; and you will be my witnesses in Jerusalem, in all Judea
and Samaria, and to the ends of the earth" (Acts 1:8). The remaining stories

show disciples obeying Jesus by proclaiming the way of the reign of God and healing people throughout the world. The Acts of the Apostles tells of Jesus' many disciples, who, in the power of the Holy Spirit, do and say what Jesus did. Peter and John do this first in Jerusalem, where they heal a lame man near the Temple. Philip teaches and baptizes people in Samaria. Dorcas helps the poor in Judea, and when she dies, Peter presents her alive again. John goes to Ephesus and is exiled to the island of Patmos, where he writes to the seven churches in Asia Minor (Turkey). At the end of his writing, which is called the Revelation to John, he presents his vision of the reign of God: a new heaven, a new earth, and a new Jerusalem.

The decision to journey on the way of the reign of God is for us too. We also are invited to follow Jesus, to receive and enter the kingdom of God, and in the power of the Holy Spirit, to live as signs of God's reign throughout the world.

Worship Center Order

PREPARATION FOR WORSHIP

The children's worship leader and the greeters arrive at the center at least fifteen minutes before the children. The greeters make final preparations of the room and the feast. The leader prepares by sitting on the circle on the floor, praying and becoming centered in God in order to feel ready when the children arrive. The greeters meet the children outside the door, where they help the children prepare to enter this special place to be with God.

WE APPROACH GOD

The Greeting

Greet each child as he or she sits down on the circle. When everyone is present, say, in a quiet voice:

Welcome to this special place to be with God. Here we can listen to God, hear stories of God, and talk with God. We do not have to hurry anymore because we have all the time we need. And we can talk more softly because someone might be talking with God and we do not want to disturb them. Now let us worship God by greeting each other.

The leader and children say and sign the following:

L: The Lord be with you.
C: And also with you.

During Easter, use this greeting:

L: Christ is risen!
C: Christ is risen indeed! Alleluia, alleluia!

Songs of Praise

Sing songs of praise to God. These should be meditative songs that help prepare the group to listen to God. End by saying quietly:

God asks us to become quiet within so we can hear God speaking to us. Let's sing the words God says to us.

Sing and sign "Be Still and Know That I Am God" or other meditative songs.

WE PROCLAIM GOD'S WORD

Telling God's Word

When you have finished singing, say:

Now it is time to listen to one of God's stories. Watch closely where I go, so you will know where the [say the name of the presentation] lives.

> *Go to the "**Presentations**" section in this book, and find the story or parable for the session; use it after the prayer for illumination, below.*

Prayer for Illumination

Before you begin telling the story sit back and say:

Let's sing the prayer of illumination to ask God to help us say what God wants us to say and hear what God wants us to hear.

Sing "May the Words of My Mouth," by John Bell (GIA Publications). Then sit back, pause, and proceed to tell the story or parable.

Responding to God's Word:
Wondering Together

In the worship center, the response to God's word takes two forms: (1) the use of wondering questions to continue engaging the story as a group, and (2) the use of the story materials and art materials for the children's personal responses. Wondering questions are suggested at the end of each presentation. There are more questions than you can use in a session, so choose only a few to use. When you have finished wondering together, say:

Watch closely how I put these materials away, so they will be ready when you want to use them next.

Place the materials back in their baskets and tray or box in reverse order. Do this slowly and respectfully, as though they are your friends. Be silent, so the children will watch what you do. By watching, they are learning how to put the materials away themselves. When all the materials are on the tray or in a parable box, say:

Watch closely where I go, so you will know where the [say the name of the story or parable] lives. You might want to use them for your work today.

Walk silently and slowly to the shelf, carrying the materials carefully with both hands. Return silently to the circle and sit down. Remain centered in God.

Responding to God's Word: Story and Art Materials

Say in a quiet voice:

I wonder what you would like to do today that shows how you feel about this story. Or perhaps there are other stories you would like to work with or unfinished work you have from another time.

Ask the child to your right what he or she would like to do. That child goes and gets a rug, places it where he or she would like to work, and then gets the materials. As soon as the first child leaves the circle, ask the next child. Continue until all have decided what they would like to do. Tell those who are unable to choose at first that you will come back to them or to hold up their hand when they know what they want to do. The children work independently or cooperatively with one or two others. They will ask if they need help. Approach children only if they are misusing the materials. You may need to retell the story to remind them how to use the materials.

Returning to the Circle

When the response time is almost over, signal with a bell or some other signal. When you have the children's attention, quietly say:

It is time to get ready for the feast. You do not have to hurry. If you are not finished with your work, you may put it in your folder. You may finish it the next time you are here.

Return to your place on the circle to be ready for the children. The greeters help those who need it. As the children are putting their things away, turn to the central shelf, behind you, and take the cloth, which should be the color of the church year season. Spread it on the floor in front of you. Place the Bible (and the children's offerings, if taken before they entered the room) on the underlay.

Reading the Bible

When the children are seated on the circle, point to the Bible and say:

This is the Bible. The story [parable] we heard today is in the Bible.

Open the Bible to the reading for the day and turn it so the children can see the words that have been highlighted with a highlighting marker. Read the words slowly and meaningfully. Then take a bookmark and say:

Here is the bookmark I will put in this place so you can find the story yourself. There is a picture of [name the picture] on it. You might want to look at these words yourself. Perhaps you would like someone to read them to you.

Put the bookmark in the Bible and place the Bible back on the cloth.

WE GIVE THANKS TO GOD

Prayer of Thanksgiving

Now it is time to give thanks to God. You can say something you are thankful for or something about the story or your work. When it is your turn, you may talk to God out loud. Or, if you don't want to talk out loud to God, just say "Amen" so we know when you are finished. Let us get ready to pray.

Say and sign these words:

L: The Lord be with you.
C: And also with you.
L: Lift up your hearts.
C: We lift them up to the Lord.
L: Let us give thanks to the Lord our God.
C: It is right to give our thanks and praise.

Engage in a time of prayer. Be at home in the silence, giving the children time to pray. When the praying is over, ask a child to return the Bible to the prayer table and the other materials to the shelf.

Preparation of the Feast

Say to the children:

Now it is time for the feast. Let's make our "tables" for the feast. [Name] will give you a large white paper napkin. Place it on the floor in front of you. Unfold it silently and slowly. Smooth it out with your hands. This will be your "table."

(For more details on the feast, see Young Children and Worship, *p. 59.)*
A child distributes napkins to the others. When all the "tables" are made, say:

Today our feast is [name the foods and the drink]. You may have [the amounts that each may take].

Children distribute the food, starting with you. Be sure to say "thank you." A greeter carries the beverage on a tray, while another offers it to each person.

The Feast

Have a joyful time of conversation as you eat. When everyone is finished, say:

Now it is time to put away our feast. Watch.

Take the cup off your napkin. Place any leftover food in the center of the napkin and gather the corners together. Put the napkin in the cup. Then a child comes with the wastebasket or tray to collect the cups. (The leader or a greeter keeps a list of the children and chooses who helps that day so eventually each child will have a turn to help.)

GO IN GOD'S NAME

After the cups are collected say:

When someone comes for you, [name the greeter] will come and tell you. I would like to say goodbye to you and give you a blessing. So first, come to me so we can say goodbye and I can bless you.

Benediction

Sing songs or talk until parents or caregivers come for the children. Then each child goes to the leader and is given a positive, personal word of blessing. Do this quietly so only the child hears. Then say:

God go with you. Go in peace to love and serve the Lord.

PRESENTATIONS

1

Baby Jesus Is Presented to God

Luke 2:22–38

Walk slowly to the shelf (see p. 11) and pick up the tray with the materials for **Baby Jesus Is Presented to God.*** *Carry it carefully to the circle, and set the tray beside you. Take the white felt circular underlay from the tray and spread it out in front of you. Smooth out the underlay as you say:*

> This is the time we celebrate the mystery that God came to us in Jesus the Christ, the Light for the whole world. Today we remember that the baby Jesus was presented to God in the Temple.

Place the Temple on the underlay about eight inches from you and to the left of center. Place Anna on the step of the Temple, to your left. Then continue:

> After Jesus was born in Bethlehem, Mary his mother . . .

Present Mary holding baby Jesus, and place them on the underlay to your far right. Later you will be moving them to the Temple. Continue, saying:

> and Joseph . . .

Present Joseph and place him to your right of Mary.

> went to the Temple in Jerusalem to present Jesus to God.

Move them a little toward the Temple.

> Now many, many years ago, God had promised to send a special child called the Christ. Year after year people waited for this gift. They would go to the Temple and ask God to send the promised Christ, who would set them free.

> Simeon was one of those who was waiting.

Present Simeon, holding him in front of you and say:

> God had said to Simeon, "I promise you, that before you die, you will see the Christ."

WARNING! Possible choking hazard! This story contains a small figure that could possibly cause choking to children putting it in their mouth. Do not use this story with children under the age of three.

Place Simeon opposite Mary to your far left on the underlay.

Then one day the Holy Spirit said to Simeon, "Go to the Temple."

Move Simeon to the left of center in front of the Temple, saving space for Anna to eventually stand opposite Joseph.

It was the same day Mary and Joseph were presenting Jesus to God.

Move Mary and Joseph to the Temple, stopping them at the right of the center with Mary facing Simeon. Joseph is to your right of Mary.

When Simeon saw the baby, he knew Jesus was the promised Christ. He held Jesus in his arms . . .

Place the baby in Simeon's arms so that Jesus' head is at Simeon's fingers and his feet are touching Simeon's body.

and thanked God, saying:
　　"Now you are letting me go in peace.
　　My eyes have seen your salvation,
　　A light for the whole world."

Pause. Return the baby to Mary. Then say:

Now there was a prophet named Anna.

Touch Anna on the back as you say:

Anna never left the Temple. Night and day she worshiped God, praying and fasting, waiting and waiting for the promised Christ, and now she was very old.

Rub Anna's back with your finger.

When Anna saw the baby . . .

Move Anna beside Simeon, opposite Joseph, facing the baby, and continue, saying:

she knew Jesus was the promised Christ. "Thank you, God," she prayed. And Anna went to tell those who were waiting,

Turn Anna and move her to the edge of the underlay to your left and say:

"The long expected Christ is born."

Move Anna in a circle, clockwise, around the underlay as you say:

"The promised Christ is here.
   Jesus the Christ has come,
   Jesus the Christ, the Light for the whole world."

Continue moving Anna until she is once again looking at Jesus.

Responding to God's Word:
Wondering Together

Now I wonder how it feels to hold this baby?

I wonder how Simeon feels as he looks at the baby?

I wonder how Simeon feels holding Jesus the Christ?

I wonder what Simeon is saying to the baby?

I wonder how Simeon knows this baby is the Christ?

I wonder how Mary feels about what Simeon said to God?

I wonder how Anna feels as she looks at the baby?

I wonder how Anna knows that Jesus is the Christ?

I wonder how Anna feels telling people that Christ has come?

I wonder why Anna is the first to go and tell that God has given the promised gift of Jesus the Christ?

I wonder if the people listen to Anna?

I wonder how Joseph feels about this baby?

I wonder how Mary feels about her baby?

> *Return to the Worship Center Order and continue. The scripture reading is Luke 2:22, 25–32*, 36–38.*

---

*Some congregations still sing the words of Simeon. If your congregation sings or says the words of Simeon called the "Song of Simeon" or *Nunc Dimittis* (Luke 2:29–32), you may wish to sing or say those words of praise with the children.

MATERIALS

1. Wooden tray
2. Two baskets for figures: one for Mary, baby Jesus, and Joseph; one for Simeon and Anna
3. White felt circular underlay: 36″ in diameter
4. Wooden figures:*   **Standing**—Mary, baby Jesus, Joseph, Simeon, Anna (**WARNING: Possible choking hazard.** The figure for Jesus is very small and not suitable for children under three years of age.)
5. Temple*
6. If you wish to teach the children the "Song of Simeon" (*Nunc Dimittis*) use one from your hymnal, your church's Book of Worship, or Luke 2:29–32 in the translation of the Bible your congregation uses.

Children

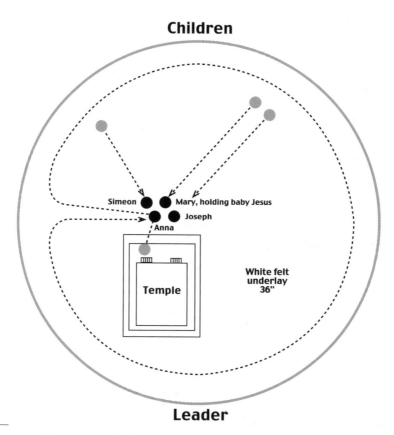

Leader

*Patterns and instructions for items marked with an asterisk, here and throughout, appear in the patterns section of this book, pp. 205–76. The colors of the felt named in the Materials sections are Rainbow Classic Felt made by Kunin Felt, Foss Manufacturing Company, 380 Lafayette Road, Hampton, NH 03843; Phone: (603) 929-6100; Fax (603) 929-6180; E-mail tjprovencal@fossmfg.com; Web address: www.kuninfelt.com (click on Product Information: Rainbow Classic Felt to view these colors). Names and colors of fabric are subject to change.

2

Follow Me

Mark 1:16–20

Walk slowly to the shelf and pick up the tray with the materials for **Follow Me.** *Carry it carefully to the circle and set the tray beside you. Take the green and blue felt underlay and lay it out in front of you, with the green closest to you. Smooth it. Then point to the place where the green and blue meet at your right, and say:*

This is the Sea of Galilee.

Trace the sea all around its edge, moving counterclockwise. Then say:

So many important things happen by the sea that we need a small piece of it to help us tell the stories.

Move your hands over the sea, portraying the following actions, with your voice full of wonder and amazement, and then with calmness as you end.

The sea is a wonderful and strange place. . . . When the wind blows . . . the sea becomes very rough and wild. And when the wind is calm . . . the sea is peaceful and still.

Pause and enjoy the calm.

Many different people live by the Sea of Galilee. Some are poor.

Present a poor woman and place her to your right.

Some are sick.

Present a sick man and place him a little to the right of the woman.

Some are children.

Present a girl and a boy and place them near the poor woman.

Some are in the fishing business.

Present Peter and say,

This is Peter.

Place Peter on the shore to the left of the poor woman. Name the other fishers as you present them. Present Andrew and place him beside Peter. Present the net, and toss it into the sea in front of them, with part of the net remaining on the shore. Place the boat in the water by the shore to the left of Peter and Andrew. Present and place James and John, their father, and the servant in the boat. A net is already in the boat. Sit back and pause a moment looking at the scene. Then present Jesus and say:

Once there was someone who came to the Sea of Galilee.

Present Jesus and place him on the underlay to the right of the sick man and say:

He said many amazing things and did such wonderful things that people followed him. He came close to the sick.

Move Jesus to the sick man.

He encouraged the poor.

Move Jesus to the poor woman.

And he enjoyed the children.

Move Jesus to the children.

"This is *the way* God wants us to care for each other," he said. "This is *the way* of the kingdom of God." But they did not understand, so he said, "Come. Follow me. I will *show* you the way. I will *show* you the way of the kingdom of God."

Move Jesus to the left of Peter and Andrew and say:

"Come. *Follow me.*"

Move Jesus ahead until he is almost to the boat. Then say:

Peter followed.

Move Peter behind Jesus, leaving room for James and John to leave the boat in front of Peter.

Andrew, Peter's brother, followed.

Move Andrew beside Peter. Then move Jesus farther, facing the boat and leaving room for James and John to stand behind Jesus after they leave the boat. Then say:

"Come. *Follow me.* I will *show* you the way of the kingdom of God." James and John followed too.

Move James out of the boat and place him behind Jesus. Then move John and place him beside James. Sit back and pause a moment.

Responding to God's Word: Wondering Together

I wonder how the poor and the sick feel near this person?

Move Jesus to the poor woman and the sick man.

I wonder what they are saying to each other?

Move Jesus to Peter and Andrew and touch their shoulders as you say their names in the next question.

I wonder why Peter and Andrew would leave their fishing nets and follow this person?

I wonder why James and John are following?

Touch James's and John's shoulders.

I wonder if these others followed?

I wonder what kind of leader this person is?

Touch Jesus' shoulder.

I wonder how this leader will treat the ones who follow him?

I wonder what the kingdom of God is like that he is showing them?

I wonder if this person has a name?

Touch Jesus' shoulder.

I wonder if it is safe to follow him?

Return to the Worship Center Order and continue. The scripture reading is Mark 1:16–20.

MATERIALS

1. Wooden tray
2. Five baskets: one for Jesus; one for the poor woman, sick man, girl, and boy; one for Peter, Andrew, James, and John; one for the father and servant; one for the fishing nets.
3. Lime green and blueberry bash felt Sea of Galilee underlay: 40" by 48". Cut a green piece of felt 40" by 24" and a blue piece of felt 40" by 24". Cut slight waves on a 40" edge of the blue felt and glue or sew it on top of a 40" edge of the green felt. (Finished size is 40" by 48".) Round off the corners.
4. Wooden figures:*　　***Sitting**—father and servant
   ***Standing**—Jesus, poor woman, sick man, girl, boy, Peter, Andrew, James, and John;
5. Fishing boat*
6. Two fishing nets (purchase a small net from a sporting goods store and trim to 15" by 15".)

Children

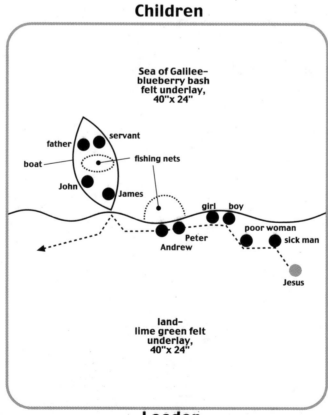

Leader

3

A New Teaching

Mark 1:21–28; Luke 4:31–37

Walk slowly to the shelf and pick up the tray with the materials for **A New Teaching.** *Carry it carefully to the circle and set the tray beside you. Take the green and blue felt underlay and lay it out in front of you, with the green closest to you. Smooth it. Then point to the place where the green and blue meet at your right, and say:*

This is the Sea of Galilee.

Trace the sea all around its edge, moving counterclockwise. Then say:

So many important things happen by the sea that we need a small piece of it to help us tell the stories.

Move your hands over the sea, portraying the following actions, with your voice full of wonder and amazement, and then with calmness as you end.

The sea is a wonderful and strange place. . . . When the wind blows . . . the sea becomes very rough and wild. And when the wind is calm . . . the sea is peaceful and still.

Pause and enjoy the calm.

Many different people live by the Sea of Galilee. Some are poor.

Present a poor woman and place her to your right.

Some are sick.

Present a sick man and place him a little to the right of the woman.

Some are children.

Present a girl and a boy and place them near the woman.

Peter and Andrew are fishermen.

65

Present Peter and Andrew. Place them to the right of where the synagogue will be placed. (Jesus will be standing at the center so people will be in two rows, with those in the back looking at Jesus between the front two.) Then say:

So are James and John.

Place James and John behind Peter and Andrew.

Some have unclean spirits.

Present the man with the unclean spirit. Continue holding him as you say:

Unclean spirits say and do things people don't like.

Place the person near the spot where the synagogue will be placed.

There is a synagogue in the village of Capernaum by the sea.

Present the synagogue, and place it near the edge of the underlay that is closest to you, toward the left corner.

A synagogue is a special place to worship God and to learn the best ways to live.

Scribes are teachers and rulers in the synagogue.

Present and place two scribes by the synagogue, one to the right and one to the left of the entrance. Pause and then say:

Once there was someone who came to the Sea of Galilee.

Present Jesus and place him on the underlay to the right of the sick person and say:

He said many amazing things and did such wonderful things that people followed him. He came close to the sick.

Move Jesus to the sick man.

He encouraged the poor.

Move Jesus to the poor woman.

And he enjoyed the children.

Move Jesus to the two children.

"This is the way God wants us to care for each other," he said. "This is the way of the kingdom of God." But they did not understand, so he said, "Come. Follow me. I will *show* you the way. I will *show* you the way of the kingdom of God."

They *followed* him to the synagogue.

Move Jesus to the entrance of the synagogue, and stand him facing the Sea.

He began teaching. "This is amazing," they said. "He is teaching in *a new way*. He teaches with *authority*, not like the scribes."

Pause.

Now the man with an unclean spirit started yelling, "What are you doing here, Jesus? Are you here to destroy us? I know who you are. You are the Christ."

Pause. Then with a firm, but centered, calm voice say:

Jesus said to the spirit, "Be still. Come out of him!" The unclean spirit began shaking the man.

Shake the man by picking him up just a little and flopping him in several fast movements. Then say:

And it left.

Let the man rest on the ground for a moment, and with your hands gently touching the sides of his body lovingly pick him up and stand him in front of Jesus.

They were amazed and kept asking, "What is this? This is a *new teaching!* Even the unclean spirits do what Jesus says."

Pause.

Responding to God's Word:
Wondering Together

I wonder how the people feel now that the unclean spirit is gone?

I wonder how this person feels to be free of the unclean spirit?

Touch the person.

I wonder how the people feel hearing the unclean spirit ask Jesus if he is here to destroy them?

I wonder how the unclean spirit knows Jesus is the Christ?

I wonder who the people think Jesus is?

I wonder how the scribes feel about Jesus when the people say Jesus teaches in *a new way*, with *authority* and not like the scribes?

I wonder what Jesus taught that was different from the scribes?

I wonder what the people think of the *way of the kingdom of God* that Jesus is showing them?

I wonder what this person will do now that the unclean spirit is no longer in him?

I wonder if Peter, Andrew, James, and John and the others still want to follow Jesus?

Return to the Worship Center Order and continue. The scripture reading is Mark 1:21–28.

MATERIALS

1. Wooden tray
2. Five baskets for figures: one for Jesus; one for the poor woman, sick man, girl, and boy; one for the man with an unclean spirit; one for two scribes; one for Peter, Andrew, James, and John
3. Lime green and blueberry bash felt Sea of Galilee underlay (Make one for this story using the directions for session 2.)
4. Wooden figures*   ***Standing***—Jesus, poor woman, sick man, girl, boy, man with an unclean spirit, two scribes, Peter, Andrew, James, and John
5. Synagogue*

Children

Leader

4

Jesus and the Paralytic
Mark 2:1–12; Matthew 9:1–8; Luke 5:17–26

Walk slowly to the shelf and pick up the tray with the materials for **Jesus and the Paralytic.** *Carry it carefully to the circle and set the tray beside you. Take the green and blue felt underlay and lay it out in front of you, with the green closest to you. Smooth it. Then point to the place where the green and blue meet at your right, and say:*

This is the Sea of Galilee.

Trace the sea all around its edge, moving counterclockwise. Then say:

So many important things happen by the sea that we need a small piece of it to help us tell the stories.

Present the house and say:

This is the house where Jesus stayed when he was in the village of Capernaum.

Place the house in front of you on the green part. Place Jesus in the back of the house, to your right. Then say:

Crowds of people followed Jesus to listen to his new teaching of the kingdom of God. Peter followed,

Present Peter and place him to the right of Jesus and continue:

Andrew followed,

Present Andrew and place him to the right of Peter and continue:

James followed,

Present James and place him to the left of Jesus and continue:

and John followed.

Present John and place him to the left of James and continue:

Many women followed.

Present and place three women to your left, in the house.

Children followed too.

Present and place the girl beside the women and the boy beside the girl and continue.

So did the poor,

Present and place a poor woman in front of the house to your right. Continue presenting the sick, lonely, rich, farmer, and fishers in front of the house placing them in a row, from your right to left as you name them.

So did the sick, and the lonely. Rich people, farmers, and fishers followed too.

Pause. Then say:

The scribes, from the synagogue, watched.

Present and place two scribes behind those named above.

So many followed there was no room left.

Pause.

Now four more were coming, carrying their friend who was paralyzed.

Pick up the mat with the paralytic on it and place it in your left hand for support in presenting him. Gently trace his body as you say:

He could not move. Night and day, he lay on his mat. People said he was paralyzed because he was a *sinner.*

Pause. Look at the crowd by the door.

His friends carried him to the roof.

Place the paralytic on the roof toward your left.

They removed part of it.

Remove the right side of the roof and say:

They lowered their friend in front of Jesus.

Lower him on the mat in front of Jesus.

Jesus said, "My son, your sins are forgiven. You are right with God and you are right with people."

Sit back and pause. Then, looking at the scribes, say:

The scribes wondered,

Touch the scribes' shoulders and continue:

"Why does Jesus say, 'your sins are forgiven'? Only God can forgive sins." Jesus answered, "I want you to know that I have *authority* to forgive sins." Then Jesus said to the man, "Stand up, take your mat, and go home." He got up.

Stand up the man.

He took his mat . . .

Roll up the mat and say:

and walked home.

Move him outside carrying his mat.

"This is amazing," the people said. "We have never seen anything like this!" And they began praising God.

Responding to God's Word: Wondering Together

I wonder why the people praised God?

I wonder what the people said or did as they praised God?

I wonder how they feel about Jesus?

I wonder how the scribes are feeling?

I wonder what they are wondering about Jesus?

I wonder how they feel about Jesus' authority?

Bring the paralytic back and ask:

I wonder how this person felt when he was paralyzed?

I wonder what the friends are like who carried this person to see Jesus?

I wonder how this person feels to have his sins forgiven?

Touch the paralytic's shoulder.

I wonder how he feels taking that first step?

I wonder how the scribes feel as they watch the person walking?

I wonder what this person will do now that he can walk?

I wonder how Peter, Andrew, James, and John feel as Jesus shows them the way of the kingdom of God?

I wonder if they will still follow Jesus?

I wonder which of the others still want to follow Jesus?

> *Return to the Worship Center Order and continue. The scripture reading is Mark 2:1–12.*

MATERIALS

1. Wooden tray
2. Five baskets for figures: one for Jesus, Peter, Andrew, James, and John; one for the three women, the girl, and the boy; one for the poor woman, sick man, lonely person, rich woman, farmer, and father and servant (fishers); one for two scribes; one for the paralytic and his mat
3. Lime green and blueberry bash felt underlay (Use directions from session 2.)
4. Wooden figures:*   **Sitting**—Jesus, Peter, Andrew, James, John, three women, girl, boy, poor woman, sick man, lonely person, rich woman, farmer, two fishers (father and servant, same as in Session 2), and two scribes
   Standing—the paralytic

5. House with removable roof*
6. Mat that will roll up, about 4½″ by 2½″ or a size that will hold the paralytic (made of tweed or material that looks like lamb's wool)

Children

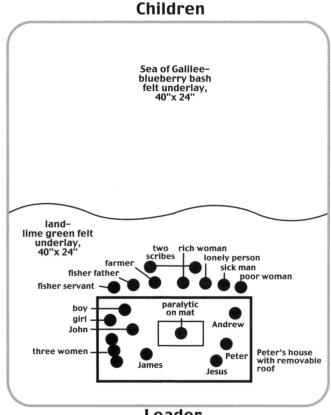

Sea of Galilee– **blueberry bash** **felt underlay,** **40″x 24″**

land– **lime green felt** **underlay,** **40″x 24″**

two scribes
rich woman
farmer
lonely person
fisher father
sick man
poor woman
fisher servant

boy
paralytic on mat
girl
Andrew
John

three women
Peter's house with removable roof
James
Peter
Jesus

Leader

5

Jesus and the Tax Collectors
Mark 2:13–17; Matthew 9:9–13; Luke 5:27–32

Walk slowly to the shelf and pick up the tray with the materials for **Jesus and the Tax Collectors.** *Carry it carefully to the circle and set the tray beside you. Take the green and blue felt underlay and lay it out in front of you, with the green closest to you. Smooth it. Then point to the place where the green and blue meet at your right, and say:*

This is the Sea of Galilee.

Trace the sea all around its edge, moving counterclockwise. Then say:

So many important things happen by the sea that we need a small piece of it to help us tell the stories.

Move your hands over the sea, portraying the following actions, with your voice full of wonder and amazement, and then with calmness as you end.

The sea is a wonderful and strange place. . . . When the wind blows . . . the sea becomes very rough and wild. And when the wind is calm . . . the sea is peaceful and still.

Pause and enjoy the calm.

One day Jesus was walking by the sea.

Place Jesus by the sea at your far right and begin moving him along the shore.

Many people were following him.

Place the crowd. See the diagram to place them. You do not want to move them again. So, while practicing where to place them, set up the last scene where Jesus is in the house with Levi. The crowd should be in front of the house looking in. Place the following as you name them.

Peter, Andrew, James, and John were following. Women were following. Children were following too. The scribes from the synagogue were watching.

74

Place the two scribes opposite where the house will be.

Now a toll road goes by the sea.

Take the sandstone felt road and roll it out starting at your left where the sea meets the green underlay. Move it at an angle that ends, about a quarter of the way in from your left, toward the top of the underlay. Place the tax collector's booth on the edge of the green and on the road (see diagram). Then say:

People pay a tax at the tax collector's booth to use this road.

Trace the booth. Then present Levi and say:

Levi was a tax collector.

Place Levi in front of the tax booth.

People did not like tax collectors. "Tax collectors are sinners," they said. So they were not supposed to walk with tax collectors. And they certainly were not to eat with them.

Sit back and pause. Then say:

Now as Jesus was teaching about the kingdom of God, he saw Levi at the tax booth.

Move Jesus toward Levi. Stand Jesus so he is looking at Levi and say:

Jesus said, "Levi, come. *Follow me.*"

Turn Jesus so he is walking on the road toward you. Then move Levi beside Jesus and say:

They walked . . .

Move Jesus and Levi along the road. When you are near the top, move them off the road to the place where the house will be placed and say:

to Levi's house . . .

Place the backdrop for the house on the felt. Then remove Jesus and Levi to the tray as you say:

to prepare a meal.

Place a round table in the center of the backdrop. Set the table with a round plate in the center and eight goblets. Place the sitting figure of Jesus between the center of the backdrop and the table; place the sitting figure of Levi to the right of Jesus. Then say:

Other tax collectors and sinners joined them.

Add six more sitting figures around the table, moving counterclockwise.

And they had a great feast.

Touch a scribe on the shoulder and say:

When the scribes saw this, they said, "*Why* is Jesus eating with tax collectors and sinners?"

Jesus answered, "People who are healthy do not need a doctor, but the sick do. I have come to ask sinners to repent, to change the way they live, and to follow the way of the kingdom of God."

Responding to God's Word:
Wondering Together

I wonder how the tax collectors and sinners feel as they sit around this table?

Make a circular motion above the table.

I wonder how Levi felt when Jesus asked him to follow him?

I wonder why Levi followed Jesus?

I wonder what Levi and Jesus are saying?

I wonder what the other tax collectors and sinners are talking about with Jesus?

I wonder who repented, who changed the ways they live?

I wonder what they will do after they change?

I wonder how Peter, Andrew, James, and John are feeling?

I wonder how the scribes and the crowd feel about what Jesus said?

I wonder what the tax collectors and sinners will do after Jesus leaves Levi's house?

I wonder what the crowd will do?

I wonder who will still follow Jesus and learn the way of the kingdom of God?

Return to the Worship Center Order and continue. The scripture reading is Mark 2:13–17.

MATERIALS

1. Wooden tray
2. Five baskets: one for Jesus and Levi, both standing and sitting figures; one for Peter, Andrew, James, John; one for a woman, boy, and girl; one for two Scribes; one for three sitting men and three sitting women. (Arrange them in the order you will be removing them from the baskets.)
3. Lime green and blueberry bash felt Sea of Galilee underlay (Use directions from session 2.)
4. Wooden figures:*   **Sitting**—Jesus, Levi, three men and three women tax collectors and sinners
   Standing—Jesus, Peter, Andrew, James, John, woman, boy, girl, two scribes and Levi
5. Sandstone felt road*
6. Tax booth*
7. Wooden backdrop*
8. Round, solid wood table, 6¾" in diameter and ¾" thick
9. Round platter 4" in diameter (Try to find a brass or wooden one from a miniature dollhouse furniture store or a craft shop, or make one of clay.)
10. Eight goblets (Buy or make ones to match the platter.)

Children

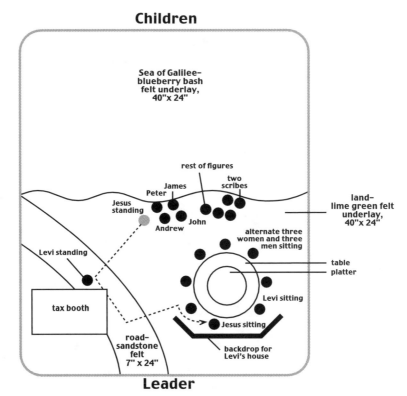

Leader

6

Jesus Calls the Twelve Disciples
Mark 3:7–19; Matthew 10:1–4; Luke 6:12–16

Walk slowly to the shelf and pick up the tray with the materials for **Jesus Calls the Twelve Disciples.** *Carry it carefully to the circle and set the tray beside you. Take the green and blue felt underlay and lay it out in front of you, with the green closest to you. Smooth it. Then point to the place where the green and blue meet at your right, and say:*

This is the Sea of Galilee.

Trace the sea all around its edge, moving counterclockwise. Then say:

So many important things happen by the sea that we need a small piece of it to help us tell the stories.

Move your hands over the sea, portraying the following actions, with your voice full of wonder and amazement, and then with calmness as you end.

The sea is a wonderful and strange place. . . . When the wind blows . . . the sea becomes very rough and wild. And when the wind is calm . . . the sea is peaceful and still.

Pause and enjoy the calm. Place the boat in the water by the shore at the center. Present the mountain and say:

There are hills and mountains around the Sea of Galilee.

Place the mountain at the center of the underlay closest to you.

One day Jesus was teaching by the sea.

Present Jesus and place him in the boat, facing the shore.

A huge crowd gathered to listen to him.

Place three groups of crowd figures on the shore, facing Jesus. Then stand the twelve disciples behind them and say:

Jesus was telling them about the kingdom of God. But they still did not understand. So Jesus said, "I will *show* you the way of the kingdom of God." Then he healed many who were sick and cast out unclean spirits.

Pause:

Then Jesus left the crowd and went up on the mountain.

Move Jesus up the mountain path at your right. At the top of the mountain turn him to face the sea.

Jesus called twelve people to be with him in a special way.

He called Peter.

Move Peter up the mountain path at your right, to the ledge below Jesus. Move him to your far left on the ledge and turn him to face Jesus. James, John, and Andrew will stand on this ledge also. Philip and the remaining seven disciples will stand on the ledge below Peter, James, John, and Andrew. Move the rest of the disciples onto the mountain as you say each one's name using the path to your right. (To help you remember the names and to provide a guide for the children, trace the shape of each disciple onto a peice of tag board and write the name of the disciple under the shape.)

Jesus called James . . . and John . . . and Andrew . . . and Philip . . . and Bartholomew . . . Levi . . . Thomas . . . James . . . Thaddaeus . . . Simon . . . and Judas.

Jesus had many other disciples, women and men and children.

Point to these in the crowd.

But these are called Jesus' twelve disciples.

Move your hand over the twelve.

These twelve disciples had been following Jesus, learning the way of the kingdom of God.

Jesus said to them: "The kingdom of God is near. Go to the villages and tell the people the way of the kingdom of God, heal the sick, and cast out unclean spirits."

The disciples left.

Move Judas and Simon down the mountain path at your right. When they are down, move them until they are near the edge of the underlay at your right and near you. (Please see the diagram: the twelve will form a rough semicircle around the mountain.)

They went through the villages,

Move Philip and Bartholomew down the mountain path at your left and to the edge of the underlay at your left and near you.

telling the good news of the kingdom of God,

Move Thaddaeus and James down the mountain path at your right and toward the edge of the underlay near the shore to your right. Then move Levi and Thomas down the mountain path at your left and toward the edge of the underlay near the shore to your left.

healing the sick,

Move Andrew and John down the mountain path at your right and near the shore, a little to the right of center.

and casting out unclean spirits

Move Peter and James down the mountain path at your left near the shore, a little to the left of center.

Responding to God's Word:
Wondering Together

I wonder why it was these people Jesus called from the crowd?

Point to the twelve disciples.

I wonder how the twelve disciples feel being called to be with Jesus?

I wonder how the twelve disciples feel about being sent to tell the good news of the kingdom of God?

I wonder what they said when they told of the kingdom of God?

I wonder how they feel being sent to heal people with all kinds of diseases?

I wonder how the disciples feel when the sick are healed?

I wonder how the people feel?

I wonder if the people want to follow the way of the kingdom of God?

Return to the Worship Center Order and continue. The scripture reading is Mark 3:13–19.

MATERIALS

1. Wooden tray
2. Two baskets for figures: one for Jesus and the twelve disciples and one for the three groups of sitting crowd figures.
3. Lime green and blueberry bash felt underlay (See directions for session 2.)
4. Boat* (See pattern for session 2.)
5. Mountain*
6. Wooden figures:*   **Sitting**—three groups of crowd figures
                        Standing—Jesus, twelve disciples

Children

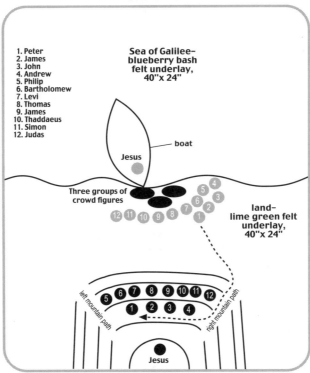

1. Peter
2. James
3. John
4. Andrew
5. Philip
6. Bartholomew
7. Levi
8. Thomas
9. James
10. Thaddaeus
11. Simon
12. Judas

Sea of Galilee–
blueberry bash
felt underlay,
40"x 24"

boat

Jesus

Three groups of
crowd figures

land–
lime green felt
underlay,
40"x 24"

left mountain path

right mountain path

Jesus

Leader

Children

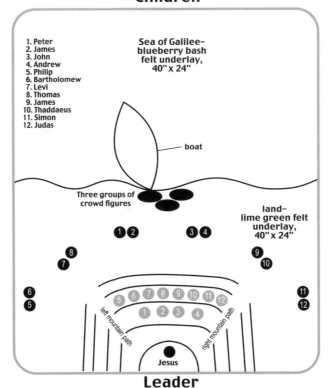

1. Peter
2. James
3. John
4. Andrew
5. Philip
6. Bartholomew
7. Levi
8. Thomas
9. James
10. Thaddaeus
11. Simon
12. Judas

Sea of Galilee–
blueberry bash
felt underlay,
40"x 24"

boat

Three groups of
crowd figures

land–
lime green felt
underlay,
40"x 24"

left mountain path

right mountain path

Jesus

Leader

7

The Parable of the Farmer and the Growing Seed

Mark 4:26–29

*Walk slowly to the shelf and pick up the **Parable of the Farmer and the Growing Seed.** Carry it carefully to the circle and place it in front of you, and say:*

I wonder if this could be a parable? It might be. Parables are very precious, like gold. And this is gold.

Gently run your hand, in a circular motion, over the lid. Then say:

This looks like a present.

Lift the box and admire it like a present and return it to the floor.

Parables are like presents. They have already been given to us. We can't buy them, or take them, or steal them. They are already ours. . . . There's another reason this might be a parable. It has a lid.

Beginning at the right-hand corner farthest from you, trace the edge of the lid with your finger, moving across the front from your right to left and continuing around the lid until you arrive where you began.

Sometimes parables seem to have lids on them. They are difficult to go into. But when you enter a parable, there is something very precious inside. . . . I know. Let's take off the lid and see if this makes a parable.

Lift the lid and peek inside. Put the lid back on and move the box to your side. Then open the lid just enough to take out the materials but not enough for the children to see inside.

(Or, if the children are familiar with the above introduction to a parable and are tired of hearing it, you could say only these words:

This looks like a parable box. I wonder if there could be a parable in it? Let's lift the lid and see if this will make a parable.)

Place the box to your side and remove the lid. Take out the antique gold underlay and smooth it and say:

I wonder what this might be? It's a mustard color. I wonder what could be so mustard?

Keep your eyes on the underlay, but as the children respond, incorporate their responses into your story. Don't discuss them. Then, still looking at the under-lay, sit back, pause, and say:

Once as Jesus was teaching beside the Sea of Galilee, he told three para-bles about seeds so the people might understand what the kingdom of God is like. He told the parable of the sower and the seeds. He told the parable of the mustard seed, and he also told this parable about a farmer and the growing seed.

Sit back and pause. Then say:

Jesus said: "The kingdom of God is like someone who scatters seed on the ground,

Take out the felt with the seeds on it and unroll it along the edge of the under-lay farthest from you, moving from your right to left. Present the farmer. Hold-ing him in your left hand, move from your right to left across the field, tracing the seed. Then say:

and goes home,

Move the farmer to the top of the underlay and take the mat from the box. Place it to the right of the farmer and say:

and sleeps,

Move the farmer to the mat, lying down. Pause for a while, letting him sleep. Then say:

and gets up,

Move the farmer up off the mat with his feet toward the center of the underlay. Pause for a while. Then say:

and sleeps,

Move the farmer onto the mat, lying down. Pause and say:

and gets up, night and day. The seed sprouts and grows, he does not know how. The earth produces of itself, first the stalk,

Roll out the felt with the green stalks on it above the seed so that the seed still

shows. Trace three of the stalks. Then sit back and pause while it grows. Then say:

then the head,

Roll out the felt with the stalks and heads on it above the felt with stalks so the stalks still show. Trace three of the heads. Sit back and pause, allowing it to grow. Then say:

then the full grain in the head.

Roll out the felt with the golden grain and trace the full grain in the head. Then say:

But when the grain is ripe, at once the farmer gathers it with his sickle, because the harvest has come."

Take the sickle from the box, place it in the farmer's hand, and move the farmer to the grain. Roll up the wheat. Place the farmer and gathered grain in the center of the underlay for wondering.

Responding to God's Word:
Wondering Together

I wonder what the farmer is doing besides sleeping and getting up while the grain is growing?

I wonder how the farmer feels trusting the seed to the earth, and the sun and the rain?

I wonder how the farmer feels about the grain as it is growing?

I wonder if the farmer pays any attention to the grain while it is growing?

I wonder how the farmer feels about the grain when it is ready to harvest?

Return to the Worship Center Order and continue. The scripture reading is Mark 4:26–29.

MATERIALS

1. Business envelope box wrapped in plain gold paper (See instructions in Appendix B.)

2. Antique gold felt underlay: 31″ by 36″
3. Farmer* (color, mount, and laminate; see instructions in Appendix D.)
4. Mat* (color, mount, and laminate; see instructions in Appendix D.)
5. Sickle* (color, mount, and laminate; see instructions in Appendix D.)
6. Four felt pieces* for the growing grain

Children

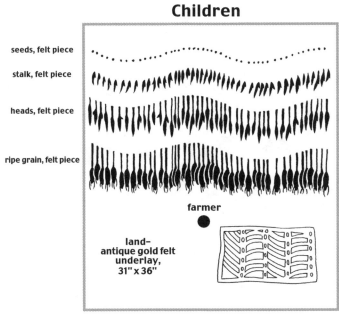

seeds, felt piece

stalk, felt piece

heads, felt piece

ripe grain, felt piece

farmer

land–
antique gold felt
underlay,
31″ x 36″

Leader

8

The Parable of the Treasure

Matthew 13:44

*Walk slowly to the shelf and pick up the **Parable of the Treasure.** Carry it care-fully to the circle and place it in front of you. Take a moment of silence to cen-ter yourself and feel the parable forming in you. Touch the lid gently, with wonder, and say:*

I wonder if this could be another parable?

Gently move your hand over the lid.

It might be. Let's lift the lid and see if this will make a parable today.

Lift the lid and peek inside. Put the lid back on and move the box to your side. Open the lid just enough to take out the materials but not enough for the chil-dren to see inside. Take out the gold felt underlay. Smooth it and, keeping your eyes on the underlay, say:

I wonder what this might be? It's such a bright gold. I wonder what could be this color?

As the children respond, keep your eyes on the underlay and incorporate their responses into your story. For example:

"It could be the sun." "It could be a balloon." "It could be a field." I wonder if there is anything else that might help us?

Take out the french vanilla felt skyline of the village and place it near the edge of the underlay nearest you (see diagram). Smooth it, and express wonder about what it might be. One at a time, take the furnishings for the house (col-ored, mounted, and laminated) and arrange them in the center "house." Take out the material for the boundary of the field (colored, mounted, and laminated). Place it along the boundary of the field, nearest the children, wondering what it might be. Sit back a moment, then say:

Once as Jesus was teaching, people began to follow him. As they followed, he told them about a special kingdom—the kingdom of God. But they did not understand. So he said:

"The kingdom of God is like treasure . . .

Take the golden treasure bag from the box, present it, and say:

hidden in a field.

Hide it in among the "stones" of the boundary of the field. Take the person out of the box and move him from the "middle house" through the field. Move him past the treasure. Stop and move back. Stop by the treasure and say:

Someone found it . . .

Take the treasure from under the rock. Hold it, look inside the bag, and smile. Then say:

and hid it again.

Joyfully hide it again. Then say:

Then with *joy* he goes and sells everything he has and buys the field."

Move the person to his house, remove the things he sells, and place them by the other houses. Then put the SOLD sign on his house and move the person back to the treasure. Take the treasure bag out and put it in the person's hands. Then keeping the bag on the person, open it to represent his looking inside. Sit back and begin the wondering.

Responding to God's Word:
Wondering Together

I wonder what is so great about this treasure that this person sold everything he owned to have it?

I wonder how he feels holding this treasure?

I wonder how long the treasure was in the field?

I wonder how many passed by it?

I wonder why this person sees the treasure and others don't?

I wonder what this person will do now?

Return to the Worship Center Order and continue. The scripture reading is Matthew 13:44.

MATERIALS

1. Business envelope box wrapped in plain gold paper
2. Gold felt underlay: 33″ by 30″
3. French vanilla felt for village:* 33″ by 18″
4. Boundary for the field* (color, mount on card stock, and laminate)
5. Beautiful golden treasure bag, made of gold cloth with sequins
6. Person who finds the treasure* (color, mount, and laminate)
7. Furnishings* for the house (color, mount, and laminate)
8. SOLD sign* (color, mount, and laminate)

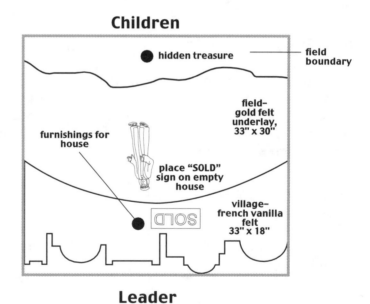

9

The Parable of the Fishnet

Matthew 13:47–48

Walk slowly to the shelf and pick up the **Parable of the Fishnet.** *Carry it carefully to the circle and place it in front of you. Take a moment of silence to center yourself and feel the parable forming in you. Touch the lid gently, with wonder and say:*

I wonder if this could be another parable?

Gently move your hand over the lid.

It might be. Let's lift the lid and see if this will make a parable today.

Lift the lid and peek inside. Put the lid back on and move the box to your side. Open the lid just enough to take out the materials but not enough for the children to see inside. Take out the blue and green underlay and place the green near you. Smooth it and express wonder about what it might be.

I wonder what could be so blue? It feels cool, like water. I wonder what it might be?

Trace the waves with your finger moving from your right to left.

Maybe they are waves. If they are waves, this might be a lake or a sea. I wonder what lives in this place?

Take the fish from the box and say:

Here are some fish. If fish live in here, it must be a lake or a sea.

Place the fish in the sea. Then sit back and say:

Once, as Jesus was teaching beside the sea, he told the people about a special kingdom—the kingdom of God. But they did not understand, so he said: "The kingdom of God is like a net. . . .

Present the net by holding the roll in one hand and rolling out some of it.

89

that was thrown into the sea.

Toss the net into the water and begin catching the fish in it.

It caught all kinds of fish.

Drag the net to gather the fish. When all the fish are in the net, say:

When the net was full, they pulled it ashore.

Drag the net ashore and let the fish fall loose from it. Place it by the shore.

They sat down, and put the good fish into baskets.

Place a basket on the green part of the underlay. Choose and present a few fish as "good" fish, and place them in the basket.

They threw out the bad."

Choose and present a few fish as "bad" fish and toss the bad fish into a pile on the shore. Continue sorting the rest of the fish. The fish all look alike or similar. You need to imagine what makes them good or bad. Then wonder together.

Responding to God's Word:
Wondering Together

I wonder how the net feels catching all kinds of fish?

I wonder how the good fish feel being in the net with the bad fish?

I wonder how they could tell which were good fish and which were bad fish?

I wonder how the good fish feel being good?

I wonder how the bad fish feel being bad?

I wonder why the good fish decided to be good fish?

I wonder why the bad fish decided to be bad fish?

I wonder how the good fish feel now that the bad fish are gone?

Return to the Worship Center Order and continue. The scripture reading is Matthew 13:47–48.

MATERIALS

1. Business envelope box wrapped in plain gold paper
2. Apple green and baby blue felt circular underlay: 36″ in diameter (Cut a piece of baby blue felt, 36″ by 18″. Cut waves on the 36″ edge of the baby blue felt. Cut a piece of apple green felt 36″ by 18″. Glue or sew the blue wavy edge on top of the green 36″ edge and cut to form a circle 36″ in diameter.)
3. A beautiful fishnet made of black and gold sparkling netting, 26″ by 19″
4. Fish* (color, mount, and laminate two of each fish)
5. Basket* (color, mount, and laminate)

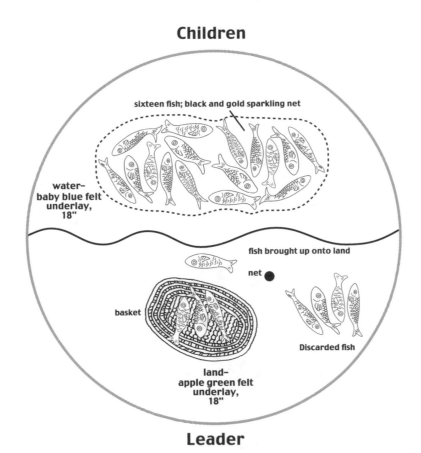

10

Jesus and the Storm

Mark 4:35–41

*Walk slowly to the shelf and pick up the tray with the materials for **Jesus and the Storm.** Carry it carefully to the circle and set the tray beside you. Take the blueberry bash felt underlay and lay it out in front of you. Smooth it and say:*

This is the Sea of Galilee.

Trace the sea along the edge, moving counterclockwise. Then say:

So many important things happen by the sea that we need a small piece of it to help us tell the stories.

Move your hands over the sea, portraying the following actions, with your voice full of wonder and amazement and then with calmness as you end.

The sea is a wonderful and strange place. . . . When the wind blows . . . the sea becomes very rough and wild. And when the wind is calm . . . the sea is peaceful and still.

Pause and enjoy the calm. Place the boat at the center of the edge near you. Place Peter, Andrew, James, John, Philip, and Thomas in the boat. Pause.

Once when Jesus was teaching beside the sea, so many people came to listen to him that he had to get into a boat to teach.

Present Jesus and place him in the stern of the boat.

He taught all day. When evening came, he was very tired. "Let's sail across the sea," he said.

Lay Jesus down on the cushion in the stern of the boat, and slowly move the boat out into the middle of the sea.

Suddenly a strong wind began to blow.

Move your hand to show the movement of the wind.

The sea became very rough and wild. Waves beat into the boat.

Raise and rock the boat as though it is being tossed by the waves.

It began filling with water.

Make motions of water going into the boat.

Jesus was still sleeping. "Wake up!" they cried. "We're drowning! Don't you care?" Jesus got up.

Stand Jesus up, and say in a firm, calm voice:

He said to the wind, "Peace! Be still!" He said to the sea, "Peace! Be still!" The wind became peaceful and still. And there was a great calm.

Pause and enjoy the calm. Then say:

"Why are you afraid?" Jesus asked his disciples. "Have you still no faith?" They were amazed and wondered, "Who is this person? Even the wind and the sea do what he says."

Responding to God's Word: Wondering Together

I wonder what it was like to be in such a great storm?

I wonder how Jesus was able to sleep during the storm?

I wonder how the wind feels blowing the sea?

I wonder how the sea feels being rough and wild?

I wonder why the wind and the sea did what Jesus said?

I wonder how the sea feels being calm?

I wonder how the disciples feel?

I wonder why the disciples are following Jesus?

I wonder if they would keep following Jesus if he were not doing amazing things?

I wonder what they told their families and friends when they came ashore?

> *Return to the Worship Center Order and continue. The scripture reading is Mark 4:35–41.*

MATERIALS

1. Wooden tray
2. Basket for figures
3. Blueberry bash felt underlay: 40″ by 36″ (Round off the corners to make it in the shape of the Sea of Galilee.)
4. Boat* (Use pattern from session 2.)
5. Cushion for Jesus to lie on in the boat, 4¼″ by 2½″
6. Wooden figures:*   **Standing**—Jesus, Peter, James, John, Andrew, Philip, and Thomas

Children

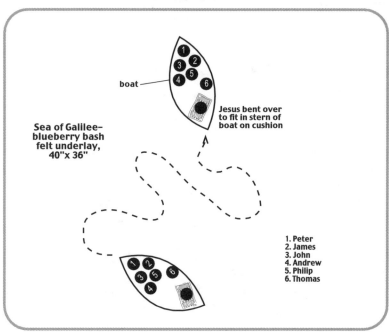

boat

Sea of Galilee–
blueberry bash
felt underlay,
40″x 36″

Jesus bent over
to fit in stern of
boat on cushion

1. Peter
2. James
3. John
4. Andrew
5. Philip
6. Thomas

Leader

11

Jesus Heals Two "Daughters"

Mark 5:21–43

Walk slowly to the shelf and pick up the tray with the materials for **Jesus Heals Two "Daughters."** *Carry it carefully to the circle and set the tray beside you. Take the green and blue felt underlay and lay it out in front of you, with the green closest to you. Smooth it. Then point to the place where the green and blue meet at your right, and say:*

This is the Sea of Galilee.

Trace the sea all around its edge, moving counterclockwise. Then say:

So many important things happen by the sea that we need a small piece of it to help us tell the stories.

Move your hands over the sea, portraying the following actions, with your voice full of wonder and amazement, and then with calmness as you end.

The sea is a wonderful and strange place. . . . When the wind blows . . . the sea becomes very rough and wild. And when the wind is calm . . . the sea is peaceful and still.

Pause and enjoy the calm.

Place Jesus, Peter, James, and John near the shore to your right. Place the backdrop for Jairus's house to your left. Place the bed in the center of the "house" with the head of the bed near the back of the backdrop. Place the mother on the left of the bed so she will be looking at her daughter. Then say:

A little girl was very sick.

Present the daughter, place her on the bed with her head near the backdrop, and continue.

She was only *twelve* years old and she was dying. Her father, Jairus,

Present Jairus and say:

was a very important man. He was a ruler of the synagogue.

Place Jairus walking toward Jesus.

When Jairus saw that Jesus had returned from across the sea, he fell at Jesus' feet pleading,

Place Jairus at Jesus' feet and continue:

"My little girl is dying. Please come. Touch her, so she will live." Jesus went with him, and a great crowd followed.

Move Jesus, Jairus, and the disciples toward the house.

Now in the crowd was a woman who had been bleeding for *twelve* years. The doctors could not heal her.

Present the bleeding woman and place her near Jesus. Continue:

But she *believed* that Jesus could. She touched the hem of his garment.

Move her behind Jesus and touch him.

Immediately the bleeding stopped. She felt well. "Who touched me?" Jesus asked. She was frightened, but she told Jesus the truth.

Move her to face Jesus.

Jesus said, "My *daughter,* your faith has made you well. You are healed. Go in peace."

Move her away from the "crowd."

Then someone came to the ruler and said, "Your daughter is dead." But Jesus said, "Don't be afraid. Believe!"

Move Jesus, Jairus, Peter, James, and John to the house. Move Jairus to his wife and Jesus to the right side of the girl. Leave room for the girl to be seen and for her to get out on the right side of the bed and move to the foot of the bed.

Jesus took her hand and said, "Little girl, get up."

Touch the girl's hand.

She got up and walked.

Raise the girl and move her to the foot of the bed.

They were overcome with amazement and joy. Jesus said, "Give her something to eat."

Responding to God's Word: Wondering Together

I wonder how she feels to be well again?

Touch the girl's arm.

I wonder how she feels as she is dying?

I wonder how the girl's mother and father feel as their daughter is dying?

Touch the mother and father.

I wonder why Jairus, a ruler of the synagogue, would ask Jesus to heal his daughter?

I wonder how Jairus feels when he hears that his daughter is dead?

I wonder how Jairus feels when Jesus says, "Don't be afraid. Believe."?

I wonder why Jesus would heal the daughter of a ruler of the synagogue when the scribes of the synagogue didn't like Jesus?

I wonder what Jairus will say to the scribes?

In Jesus' day, when a woman was bleeding people thought she was "unclean." No one was to touch her, and she was not to touch anyone.

I wonder how this woman felt for twelve years when no one would touch her, or hug her, or even be near her?

I wonder how she feels now that she is healed?

I wonder who will hug her now?

I wonder what the crowd thought when Jesus called her "daughter"?

I wonder what both daughters will do now that they are healed?

I wonder how the people feel about Jesus?

> *Return to the Worship Center Order and continue. The scripture reading is Mark 5:21–43. (Select verses to read.)*

MATERIALS

1. Wooden tray
2. Three baskets for figures: one for Jesus, Peter, James, John; one for mother, daughter, Jairus; and one for the bleeding woman
3. Lime green and blueberry bash felt Sea of Galilee underlay (Use directions from session 2.)
4. Backdrop* for Jairus's house
5. Bed: solid wood block, 4¼″ by 2¼″ and 1¼″ thick
6. White felt sheet to cover bed: 4¼″ by 2¼″
7. Wooden figures:*   ***Standing***—Jesus, Peter, James, John, mother, daughter, Jairus, and bleeding woman

Children

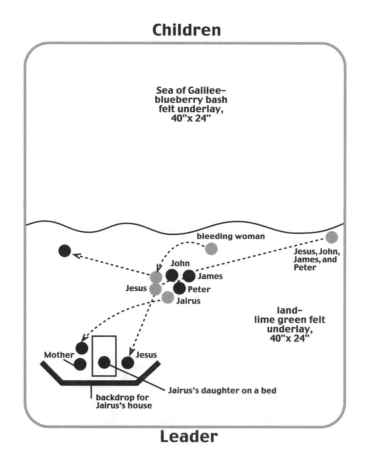

Leader

12

Jesus Feeds Five Thousand People

*Matthew 14:15–21; Mark 6:30–44; Luke 9:12–17;
John 6:1–15*

Walk slowly to the shelf and get the materials for **Jesus Feeds Five Thousand People.** *Place the tray beside you. Take the lime green underlay and smooth it out in front of you. Then present Jesus, and place him about four inches from the edge closest to you, at the center, and say:*

Jesus' disciples were coming home.

Present Judas and Simon and place them at Jesus' right. Present Philip and Bartholomew and place them at Jesus' left. (You are arranging the disciples around Jesus so they are in a position similar to the one where they were after Jesus sent them out in session 6, "Jesus Calls the Twelve Disciples." Please see the diagram.)

They had been in the villages, . . .

Present Thaddaeus and James and place them beside the disciples at the right.

healing the sick,

Present Levi and Thomas and place them beside the disciples at the left.

casting out unclean spirits,

Present Andrew and John and place them beside the disciples at the right.

and teaching the way of the kingdom of God.

Present Peter and James and place them beside the disciples at the left.

They were very tired, so Jesus said, "Let's go to a quiet place and rest."

Move Jesus forward so he is even with the first disciples.

Now many saw them going, and ran after them.

99

Move your hands and arms in an encircling motion toward the center of the underlay. The idea is to help the children feel they are a part of the crowd. Sit back and pause.

When Jesus saw the crowd, they seemed like sheep without a shepherd. So instead of asking them to leave, Jesus healed them and taught them the way of the kingdom of God.

When evening came, the disciples said to Jesus, "It's getting late. Send the crowd away so they can go to the villages and buy food." But Jesus answered, "You feed them."

Pause.

But they did not have enough food for such a huge crowd.

"What do you have?" Jesus asked.

"We have five loaves of bread and two fish."

Place a flat basket of five loaves and two fish in front of Jesus and say:

Then Jesus *took* the bread, . . .

Hold up one of the loaves in both hands.

and *blessed* it, . . .

Place your hand in blessing over the bread.

and *broke* it, . . .

Break the bread. Place it back on the basket. Break the other loaves in half. Then say:

and *gave* it to his disciples, . . .

Take the basket with the twelve tiny baskets and place it in front of you. Hold a tiny basket in front of Jesus and place a piece of the broken bread in the basket. Place it in front of Judas, the disciple closest to Jesus' right. Take another tiny basket, put another piece of bread in it, and place it in front of Philip, the disciple closest to Jesus' left. Take another basket, place bread in it, and give it to the next disciple to the right. Continue giving, back and forth, until all the bread is given. Then put a fish in a tiny basket and place the basket in front of John, the remaining disciple to Jesus' far right and repeat for James. Then say:

and the disciples gave this to the crowd.

Move Judas and the basket to the "people" to the right. Then move Philip and the basket closest to the "people" to the left. Move Simon next and then Bartholomew. Continue moving opposite disciples so that the first ten disciples almost form a circle. Then move John and James with the fish forward, completing the circle. (Moving the figures toward the children, forming a circle, allows the children to feel that they are part of the crowd being fed.)

The people ate until they were full, and there was bread left over. More than five thousand people had eaten.

The people said, "This certainly is the Christ." And they wanted to make Jesus their king. But Jesus slipped away.

Place Jesus back on the tray. Pause. Then return Jesus to the underlay for the wondering.

Responding to God's Word: Wondering Together

I wonder how the disciples are feeling about what just happened?

I wonder how the crowd feels?

I wonder why the crowd thinks Jesus is the Christ?

I wonder why the people want to make Jesus their king?

I wonder what kind of king Jesus would be?

I wonder why Jesus slipped away?

> *Return to the Worship Center Order and continue. The scripture reading is Mark 6:30–31, 41–44, and John 6:14–15.*

MATERIALS

1. Wooden tray
2. Three baskets: one for Jesus and twelve disciples; one for twelve tiny baskets; one for bread and fish
3. Lime green felt underlay: 34" by 36" with rounded corners
4. Wooden figures:* **Standing**—Jesus and the twelve disciples
5. Round, flat basket or tray on which to lay the bread and fish in front of Jesus, about 3" in diameter
6. Twelve tiny, woven, oval-shaped baskets to hold the bread and fish: about 1½" long, by 1" wide, by ¾" high (They can be found in craft shops. They come with handles, which should be removed.)

7. Five loaves of bread made of Play-Doh or nontoxic mounting putty
8. Two fish made of Play-Doh

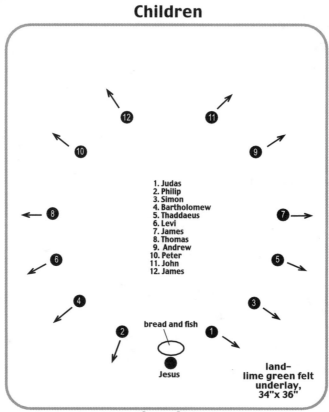

Children

1. Judas
2. Philip
3. Simon
4. Bartholomew
5. Thaddaeus
6. Levi
7. James
8. Thomas
9. Andrew
10. Peter
11. John
12. James

bread and fish

Jesus

land–
lime green felt
underlay,
34"x 36"

Leader

13

The Transfiguration of Jesus

*Matthew 16:13–23, 17:1–13; Mark 8:27–29; 9:2–8;
Luke 9:18–36*

Walk slowly to the shelf and pick up the tray with the materials for **The Transfiguration of Jesus.** *Carry it carefully to the circle and set the tray beside you.
Take the kelly green underlay and lay it out in front of you. Smooth it. Present
the figure of Jesus and say:*

Jesus and his disciples were teaching in the villages and the countryside.

*Place Jesus near the right corner that is farthest from you, leaving room for the
disciples to be placed in front of him. Present and place the disciples near
Jesus, facing him with John, Peter, and James in the row closest to Jesus.
(Please see the diagram.)*

Jesus had been saying amazing things and doing many wonderful things,
but people still did not know who he really was.

So one day, Jesus asked his disciples, "Who do people say that I am?" They
answered, "Some say you are John the Baptist, or Elijah, or one of the
prophets."

Pause. Then continue:

"But who do *you* say that I am?" Jesus asked.

Pause. Then continue:

"You are the Christ," Peter answered.

"You are blessed, Peter," Jesus said, "for God has shown you who I am."

Pause.

Then Jesus said, "I must go up to Jerusalem for Passover. I will be killed, but
on the third day God will make me alive again." The disciples could not
believe this.

Jesus taught them for six more days. Then he led Peter, James, and John to
a high mountain to talk with God.

Present the mountain and place the back edge of the mountain on the edge of the underlay closest to you and about four inches from the left side edge. Turn Jesus and move him to the foot of the mountain. Move Peter until he is behind Jesus. Then move James and John behind Peter. Move Jesus up the mountain to the center top, and turn him so he faces where Peter will stand. Move Peter to a lower ledge on the mountain, so he faces Jesus. Move James a little behind and to your left of Peter. Move John to your right of Peter. Pause. Then say:

As Jesus was talking with God, he was transfigured. His face began to shine as bright as the sun.

Glide your hand in front of his face, making sure not to touch it.

His clothes became dazzling white.

Glide your hand down in front of his clothes.

And Elijah . . .

Place and keep your right-hand fingers on the spot to Jesus' right.

and Moses . . .

Place and keep your left hand fingers on the spot to your left of Jesus. Leave both hands there as you say:

appeared beside Jesus.
Suddenly a cloud covered them.

Bring your arms and hands together, forming a circular cloud covering the scene and say:

The disciples were terrified.

Pause.

Then a voice said, "This is my special child, whom I love. Listen to him."

Slowly move your hands and arms away in a circular motion and continue:

Looking around, the disciples saw only Jesus. "Don't be afraid," Jesus said. "Come, follow me."

Responding to God's Word:
Wondering Together

I wonder how Peter, James, and John are feeling?

I wonder what they might really want to do?

I wonder what it was like to see Jesus transfigured?

I wonder how Peter, James, and John feel about what they saw?

I wonder how the disciples feel when Peter says Jesus is the Christ?

Move your hand toward the other nine disciples.

I wonder what the other disciples might have answered?

I wonder how they could know that Jesus is the Christ?

I wonder how Jesus is feeling?

Return to the Worship Center Order and continue. The scripture reading is Mark 8:27–29; 9:2–8.

MATERIALS

1. Wooden tray
2. Two baskets for figures: one for Jesus, Peter, James, and John; one for other disciples
3. Kelly green felt underlay: 36" by 36"
4. Wooden figures:*   **Standing**—Jesus, Peter, James, John, and other disciples
5. Mount of Transfiguration*

HOW THE CHURCH CELEBRATES THE TRANSFIGURATION OF JESUS

The transfiguration of Jesus is so important to the church that it is celebrated every year. It marks a turning point in the ministry of Jesus, when he leaves Galilee and begins his last journey to Jerusalem.

In most church year calendars Transfiguration Sunday is the last Sunday after Epiphany, which is the Sunday before Lent begins. However, the traditional date of the feast of the Transfiguration is August 6. You may want to tell this story on those days. If so, you may want to use one of the following introductions to this story.

This is Transfiguration Sunday, the time we celebrate the mystery that the light of God's glory shone in the face of Jesus the Christ. It was like this:

or

This is the Feast Day of the Transfiguration of Jesus. It is the day we celebrate the mystery that the light of God's glory was seen in the face of Jesus the Christ. It was like this:

Then continue with the story.

Children

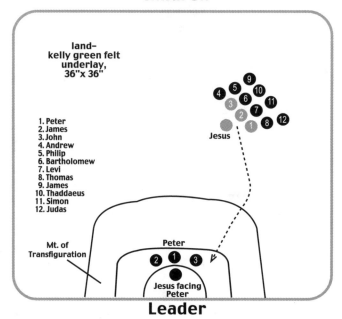

land–
kelly green felt
underlay,
36"x 36"

1. Peter
2. James
3. John
4. Andrew
5. Philip
6. Bartholomew
7. Levi
8. Thomas
9. James
10. Thaddaeus
11. Simon
12. Judas

Jesus

Mt. of
Transfiguration

Peter

Jesus facing
Peter

Leader

14

Jesus Heals a Boy

Matthew 17:14–21; Mark 9:14–29; Luke 9:37–42

*Walk slowly to the shelf and pick up the tray with the materials for **Jesus Heals a Boy**. Carry it carefully to the circle and set the tray beside you. Take the kelly green underlay and lay it out in front of you. Smooth it. Place the back edge of the Mount of Transfiguration on the edge of the underlay closest to you and about four inches from the left side edge. Place the rest of the disciples and the father and son in the right-hand corner farthest from you. (Please see the diagram. The placement is important to the moving at the end of the story.) Pause, sit back, then say:*

Jesus,

Present Jesus and place him below the mountain, approaching the crowd.

Peter,

Present and place Peter behind Jesus.

James,

Present and place James to your left of Peter.

and John

Present and place John on the other side of Peter.

are returning from the mountain where Jesus was transfigured. A man came running toward Jesus.

Move the father, rapidly, to Jesus and say:

"My son has a spirit," he cried. "It won't let him speak. It seizes him and throws him down. Your disciples could not cast it out."

Pause.

"Bring him to me," Jesus said.

Move the boy from the rest of the disciples to Jesus.

When the spirit saw Jesus, it began throwing the boy.

Tumble the boy and roll him around on the ground. Then say:

"How long has he been like this?" Jesus asked.

"Since a child. The spirit tries to kill him by throwing him into fire or water. Please help us."

Then Jesus said, "You, spirit that keeps this boy from speaking and hearing, I command you, come out of him, and never enter him again!"

The spirit began screaming and terribly tossing the boy.

Tumble the boy; then leave him lying still on the ground. Sit back and say:

The spirit left.

Pause. Then say:

But the boy looked dead. "He's dead! He's dead!" many cried.

Move Jesus to the boy and say:

Then Jesus took his hand,

Take the boy's hand. Then say:

and lifted him up . . .

Lift the boy up and say:

and he was able to stand.

Pause.

All were amazed and wondered.

Pause. Move the father and son behind the disciples to the right corner. Turn Jesus toward the disciples and say:

Later, Jesus again told his disciples, "We are going to Jerusalem for Passover. I will be killed, but on the third day God will make me alive again." They did not understand. But with Jesus leading the way, they followed him on the way to Jerusalem.

Move Jesus to your far left. Move Peter and James together until they are behind Jesus. (Please see the diagram.) Move John and disciple 4 until they are behind Peter and James. Move disciples 8 and 12; then 7 and 11, to continue the line following Jesus. Disciples 5, 6, 9, and 10 do not move, because they should already be in line with the others. Pause, and then begin the wondering.

Responding to God's Word:
Wondering Together

I wonder what it was like for this boy to have a spirit that threw him around and tried to kill him?

I wonder how the boy feels being free of the spirit?

I wonder how the father feels when his son looks dead?

I wonder how the father feels as Jesus lifts the boy up and he can stand?

I wonder how the boy feels about Jesus?

I wonder if the boy and Jesus talked with each other and what they might have said?

I wonder who the boy thinks Jesus is?

I wonder what the disciples are wondering when they see the boy is alive and standing?

I wonder how Jesus' disciples feel about what happened?

I wonder how Jesus' disciples are feeling as they follow Jesus to Jerusalem?

I wonder what the disciples might be talking about?

Return to the Worship Center Order and continue. The scripture reading is Mark 9:17–27.

MATERIALS

1. Wooden tray
2. Three baskets for figures: one for Jesus, Peter, James, and John; one for the rest of the disciples; one for the father and son
3. Kelly green felt underlay: 36″ by 36″
4. Wooden figures:*   **Standing**—Jesus, Peter, James, and John, rest of the disciples, father, and son

5. Mount of Transfiguration*

Children

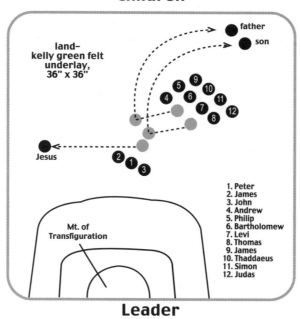

Children

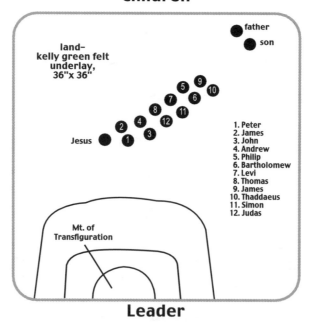

15

Who Is the Greatest?

Mark 9:33–37

Walk slowly to the shelf and pick up the tray with the materials for **Who Is the Greatest?** *Carry it carefully to the circle and set the tray beside you. Take the green and blue felt underlay and lay it out in front of you, with the green part closest to you. Smooth it. Then point to the place where the green and blue meet at your right and say:*

This is the Sea of Galilee.

Trace the sea all around its edge, moving counterclockwise. Then say:

So many important things happen by the sea that we need a small piece of it to help us tell the stories.

Move your hands over the sea, portraying the following actions, with your voice full of wonder and amazement, and then with calmness as you end.

The sea is a wonderful and strange place. . . . When the wind blows . . . the sea becomes very rough and wild. And when the wind is calm . . . the sea is peaceful and still.

Pause and enjoy the calm. Then place Peter's house near the center back. Sit back and pause.

Jesus and his disciples were returning to Capernaum.

Present them and place them in or by the house.

When they got home, Jesus asked them, "What were you arguing about on the way?" But no one would answer.

Pause for silence.

They had been arguing about who of them was the greatest.

Pause. Then say slowly:

Then Jesus said, "If you want to be the greatest, you must be last of all. If you want to be the greatest, you must be servant of all." Then he took a little child into his arms and said,

Present the child. Place the child by Jesus and slowly say:

"Whoever welcomes a child in my name welcomes me. Whoever welcomes me welcomes not me but God who sent me."

Responding to God's Word: Wondering Together

I wonder how the disciples are feeling as they argue over who is the greatest of them all?

I wonder how Jesus feels when he hears them arguing?

I wonder why they would not answer Jesus when he asks them what they were arguing about?

I wonder what they think it is like to be the greatest?

I wonder how they feel when Jesus says that the one who wants to be greatest must be last of all?

I wonder how they feel when Jesus says that the greatest must be a servant of all?

I wonder how the child feels in Jesus' arms?

I wonder how the child feels when Jesus says, "Whoever welcomes a child welcomes me and God who sent me?"

I wonder how the disciples feel about what Jesus said?

I wonder how the disciples feel about this child?

I wonder how welcoming a child is welcoming Jesus?

I wonder how this child feels about welcoming other children?

I wonder how welcoming Jesus is welcoming God?

Return to the Worship Center Order and continue. The scripture reading is Mark 9:33–37.

MATERIALS

1. Wooden tray
2. Two baskets for figures: one for Jesus and the child; one for the twelve disciples
3. Lime green and blueberry bash felt Sea of Galilee underlay (See directions for session 2.)
4. Wooden figures:*   ***Sitting***—Jesus, twelve disciples, and a child
5. Peter's house* (use pattern from session 4)

Children

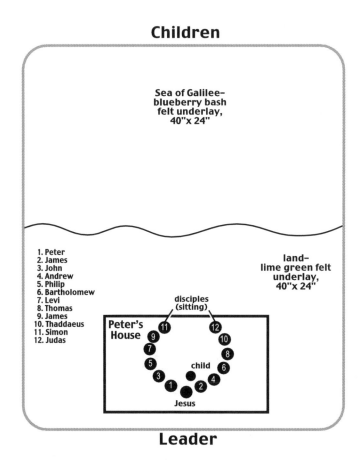

Leader

16

Jesus Makes Lazarus Alive Again

John 11

Walk slowly to the shelf and pick up the tray with the materials for **Jesus Makes Lazarus Alive Again.** *Carry it carefully to the circle and set the tray beside you. Take the silver gray felt underlay and spread it out in front of you. Smooth it. Place the backdrop and the bed on the underlay to the left of center and close to the edge nearest you. Place Mary to the left of the bed and place Martha beside her, with both facing the bed. Place the tomb a little to the right of center, at the back of the underlay (the part closest to you). Place the stone that will close the tomb beside the entrance. Sit back and pause. Then say:*

Lazarus was very sick.

Present Lazarus and place him on the bed.

He was dying. Now Jesus loved Lazarus very much. So his sisters, Mary and Martha, sent for Jesus.

Touch Mary and Martha.

But before Jesus came, Lazarus died.

They washed his body.

Pretend to wash his body.

Then they anointed it.

Put sweet-smelling anointing ointment on Lazarus.

And wrapped it in linen cloth.

Place the square linen cloth over Lazarus's head. Take the other cloth and unfold it about six inches. Lay the neck of the body on the top edge of the cloth and about five inches from the end of it. Bring the edge of the cloth over the body. Turn the bottom of the cloth up so the feet are covered. Then wrap the body with the remaining cloth. Hold the body in the palm of your left hand, with the feet at your fingertips. Place your right hand under your left and say:

They placed him in a tomb.

Slowly "carry" Lazarus to the tomb. With your right hand place him in the tomb. Roll the stone to cover the entrance. Sit back and pause. Then present Jesus and walk him from your far right to the tomb. Stop him there and say:

When Jesus arrived, Lazarus had been in the tomb for four days. Martha went to meet him,

Move Martha to Jesus.

and said, "If you had been here my brother would not have died." Jesus said to her, "Your brother will be alive again. . . . I am the resurrection and the life. Those who believe in me will live, even when they die. Do you believe this?"

"Yes," Martha said, "I believe you are the *Christ.*"

Then Mary came.

Move Mary to Jesus and pretend there is a crowd (with a hand motion) when you say:

And a crowd followed. Jesus said, "Remove the stone."

Remove the stone.

Jesus looked up and prayed, "Thank you, God, for hearing me." Then Jesus shouted, "Lazarus, come out!"

Pause.

Lazarus came out.

Take Lazarus out of the tomb.

They unwrapped him.

Unwrap Lazarus and place him near Jesus.

Now many believed that Jesus was the Christ, but some of the chief priests and scribes and others did not. They began looking for a way to arrest Jesus.

Responding to God's Word:
Wondering Together

I wonder how Mary feels when her brother is so sick?

I wonder how Martha feels?

I wonder how Martha and Mary feel as they watch Lazarus die?

I wonder what they might be saying to each other as they prepare Lazarus's body to be placed in the tomb?

I wonder how they feel that Jesus didn't come before Lazarus died?

I wonder how they feel when they see Jesus?

I wonder how they feel when Lazarus is alive again?

I wonder why Jesus loves Lazarus, Martha, and Mary? (Wonder about each one.)

I wonder why Martha, Mary, and Lazarus love Jesus? (Wonder about each one.)

I wonder how Martha knows Jesus is the Christ?

I wonder who Mary thinks Jesus is?

I wonder who Lazarus thinks Jesus is?

I wonder why some of the people love Jesus and follow him?

I wonder why some of them will not follow Jesus?

Return to the Worship Center Order and continue. The scripture reading is John 11. (Select verses to read.)

MATERIALS

1. Wooden tray
2. Two baskets: one for Jesus, Mary, Martha, and Lazarus; one for water jar, anointing oil, cotton balls, and linen cloths
3. Silver gray felt underlay: 36" by 24"
4. Wooden figures:* **Standing**—Jesus, Mary, Martha, and Lazarus
5. Backdrop for house* (Same pattern as in session 11.)
6. Bed: solid block of wood, 4½" long by 2¾" wide by 1¼" thick
7. White felt sheet to cover bed: 4¼" by 2¾"
8. Tomb:* large enough to put Lazarus's figure inside
9. Large stone to roll in front of the opening in the tomb
10. Cotton balls for washing and anointing Lazarus

11. Water jar (purchase from miniature doll house shop)
12. Sweet-smelling anointing ointment to rub on Lazarus (purchase from religious book store)
13. White, square linen cloth to place over Lazarus's head: 4″ by 4″
14. White linen cloth to wrap Lazarus's body: 16″ long by 6″ wide. (Fold it every 2″ so you can unfold it to wrap Lazarus.)

Children

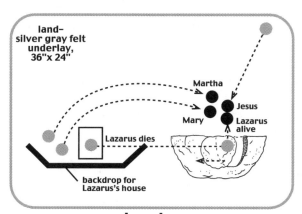

Leader

17

The Parable of the Two Sons
Matthew 21:28–32

Walk slowly to the shelf and pick up **The Parable of the Two Sons.** *Carry it carefully to the circle, place it in front of you, and say:*

> This looks like a parable box. I wonder if there could be a parable in it. Let's lift the lid and see if this will make a parable.

Place the box to your side. Open the lid of the box enough to take out the materials, but not enough for the children to see inside. Take out the antique white vineyard underlay, and place it in front of you. Smooth it and say:

> I wonder what this might be? These look like grapes so it must be a vineyard.

Trace some of the grapes with your finger. Then take the baskets from the box and place them at either edge of the entrance to the vineyard. Sit back, pause, and looking at the vineyard, say:

> Once every year the people of God go up to Jerusalem to celebrate the feast of the Passover, to remember how God led them through the waters to freedom. And every year Jesus and his family and friends went to Jerusalem to celebrate the feast. But this year as Jesus is teaching in the Temple, the chief priest and the elders are trying to trick Jesus. They ask him, "Who gave you *authority* to say what you say and do what you do?" Jesus would not answer them, instead he told them this parable. "A man . . .

Present the father and place him in the center of the vineyard.

> had two sons.

Present the first son and place him to your right, outside the vineyard. Present the second son and place him to the left, opposite the first son.

> He went to the first and said,

Move the father to the son on your right.

"Son, go work in the vineyard today."

But the son said, "No, I don't want to."

Move the father back to the center of the vineyard. Pause awhile.

Later he was sorry, so he went.

Move the first son to the vineyard and place him to the father's right. Pause. Then have him begin to pick grapes and place them in the basket at the edge of the vineyard.

The father went to the other son and said,

Move the father to the second son.

"Son, go work in the vineyard today."

"Yes, I'll go," he said.

Move the father back to the vineyard and pause, waiting. After a while, move the first son beside the father and point to the empty space to the left of the father and say:

But he didn't.

Sit back and pause. Keeping your eyes on the underlay, say:

Then Jesus asked the priests and elders, "Which of the two sons did what his father wanted?"

"The first," they answered.

Then Jesus said to them, "The tax collectors and the sinners are going into the kingdom of God before you. John the Baptist came to show you the right way to live, and you did not believe him. But the tax collectors and sinners did. They changed their ways. And even when you saw that the tax collectors and sinners had changed, you did not change and live the way of the kingdom of God."

Responding to God's Word:
Wondering Together

I wonder how the priests and elders are feeling about Jesus' parable?

I wonder how the priests and elders feel about the two sons?

I wonder how the father feels about his two sons?

I wonder what it's like for them to work in this vineyard?

I wonder how the first son feels when his father tells him to work in the vineyard?

I wonder why he said no?

I wonder how the father feels when his son said no?

I wonder how the father feels when his son comes to the vineyard?

I wonder how the son feels working with his father?

I wonder how the father feels waiting for his second son to come to the vineyard?

I wonder why the son said yes, but didn't go to the vineyard?

I wonder if this son will ever change his mind and go to the vineyard?

I wonder how the brothers feel about each other?

I wonder how Jesus feels when the priests and elders keep trying to trick him?

I wonder why the priests and elders didn't believe John the Baptist and change the way they live?

I wonder what the priests and elders wonder about this parable?

Return to the Worship Center Order and continue. The scripture reading is Matthew 21:28–32.

MATERIALS

1. Business envelope box covered with plain gold paper
2. Antique white felt underlay for vineyard, 28″ by 36″
3. Vineyard*
4. Father, two sons, and two baskets* (color, mount, and laminate)

Children

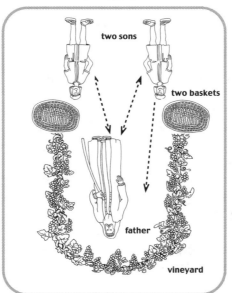

two sons

two baskets

father

vineyard

land–
antique white
felt underlay,
28"x 36"

Leader

18

The Most Important Commandment
Mark 12:28–34

Walk slowly to the shelf and pick up the tray with the materials for **The Most Important Commandment.** *Carry it carefully to the circle and set the tray beside you. Take the Jerusalem underlay and lay it out in front of you. Smooth it and trace the city with your finger as you say:*

This is the city of Jerusalem. So many important things happen in Jerusalem that we need a small piece of it to help us tell the stories.

Place the Temple at the center of the underlay, close to the edge nearest you. Pause and say:

Once every year the people of God go up to Jerusalem to celebrate the feast of the Passover, to remember how God led them through the waters to freedom. And every year Jesus and his family and friends went to Jerusalem to celebrate the feast. But this year, when Jesus entered Jerusalem, the whole city was asking, "Who is this man? Who is Jesus?"

Present and place Jesus, sitting in front of the Temple. Present and place Peter to your right of Jesus. Present and place John to the left of Jesus. Present and place James to the right of Peter.

Now as Jesus was teaching at the Temple, the chief priests . . .

Present a chief priest and place him beside John.

and the elders . . .

Present an elder and place him beside the priest.

were trying to trick Jesus. They wanted to arrest Jesus and have him killed. They kept asking, "Who gave you authority to say what you say and do what you do?" And they kept on questioning him. Then one of the teachers of the law came.

Present a teacher of the law and stand him near James, facing Jesus, and continue:

He asked Jesus, "Of all the commandments, of all the ten best ways to live, which is the most important?"

Jesus answered, "The most important commandment is this: 'Our God is one.

Place a white felt circle at the center of the underlay and continue.

Love God with all your heart . . .

Place the red felt heart on the circle.

and with all your soul, and with all your mind, and with all your strength.'

Place the half-heart shaped card with the above words on the red heart.

The second is this: 'Love your neighbor as yourself.'

Place the other half-heart shaped card with the above words on the red heart.

There is no greater commandment than these."

"You are right," the scribe said. "God is one. To love God with all your heart, with all your understanding and with all your strength, and to love your neighbor as yourself is more important than all burnt offerings and sacrifices." Jesus said to him, "You are not far from the kingdom of God."

Pause.

And from then on, no one dared to question the authority of Jesus.

**Responding to God's Word:
Wondering Together**

I wonder how Jesus feels when the people in Jerusalem wonder who he is?

I wonder how the people in Jerusalem feel as they listen to Jesus' teachings?

I wonder how the crowds feel when they hear the priests and scribes trying to trick Jesus with their questions?

I wonder how the priests and elders feel as Jesus tells what is the most important commandment?

I wonder how they feel when they hear Jesus say the second most important commandment is to "love your neighbor as yourself"?

I wonder why it is hard for some of them to love Jesus?

I wonder how Jesus feels about the priests and elders?

I wonder how the people feel when they love God with all their hearts, with all their souls, with all their minds, and with all their strength?

Return to the Worship Center Order and continue. The scripture reading is Mark 12:28–34.

MATERIALS

1. Wooden tray
2. Two baskets: one for Jesus, Peter, James, and John; one for priest, elder, and teacher of the law
3. Sandstone Jerusalem underlay (See diagram.)
4. Temple* (Use pattern from session 1)
5. Wooden figures:* **Sitting**—Jesus, Peter, James, John, a chief priest, and an elder
   Standing—a teacher of the law
6. White felt circle: 11″ in diameter
7. Red felt heart*
8. White heart-shaped card* with the Greatest Commandment on the left half and the second on the right half (mount, laminate, and cut in half)

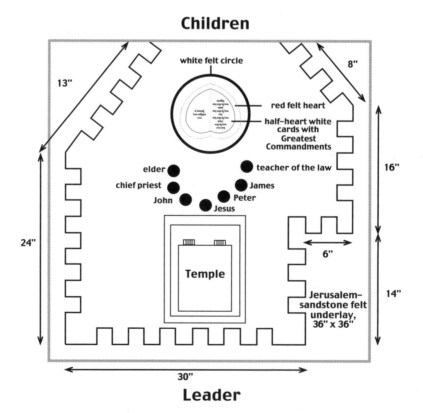

Children

white felt circle

red felt heart

half-heart white cards with Greatest Commandments

elder · chief priest · John · Jesus · Peter · James · teacher of the law

Temple

Jerusalem–sandstone felt underlay, 36″ x 36″

13″ 8″ 16″ 6″ 14″ 24″ 30″

Leader

19

The Gift of the Poor Widow
Mark 12:41–44

Walk slowly to the shelf and pick up the tray with the materials for **The Gift of the Poor Widow.*** *Carry it carefully to the circle and set the tray beside you. Take the Jerusalem underlay and lay it out in front of you. Smooth it and say:*

This is the city of Jerusalem.

Trace the outer edges of the underlay with your finger, moving counterclockwise, and continue.

So many important things happen in Jerusalem that we need a small piece of it to help us tell the stories.

Place the Temple at the center of the underlay near the edge closest to you. Place the offering chest (treasury) with some coins in it on the underlay opposite the Temple, leaving room for figures to sit and move between it and the Temple. Place a chief priest on one side of the chest and an elder on the other side. Sit back a moment, and then say:

Once every year the people of God go up to Jerusalem to celebrate the feast of the Passover, to remember how God led them through the waters to freedom, and every year Jesus

Present Jesus and place him sitting in front of the Temple, opposite the treasury.

and his family and friends go up to Jerusalem to celebrate the feast.

Present and place Peter to Jesus' right. Present and place John to Jesus' left. Present and place James beside Peter.

This year Jesus was at the Temple watching the crowd put their offerings into the Temple treasury. Many rich people threw in lots of money.

WARNING! Possible choking hazard! This story contains coins that could possibly cause choking to children putting them in their mouth. Do not use this story with children under the age of three.

Present a rich woman. Set the rich woman on the underlay to your right and pick up some coins. Then move the person to the treasury and drop in each coin so you can hear it land. Then move the person to the far left. Repeat this with the second rich woman, the rich boy, the rich girl, and the rich man.

Then a poor widow came.

Present the widow. Set her to your right and pick up two very small copper coins. Move her to the treasury.

She put in two very small copper coins, not even worth a penny.

Drop in the two copper coins, one at a time.

Jesus said to his disciples, "Listen. This poor widow has put more into the offering than all the others. They gave out of their wealth. She gave out of her poverty. She put in everything. She gave all she had to live on."

Responding to God's Word:
Wondering Together

I wonder how Jesus feels watching the people put their offering into the Temple treasury?

I wonder how the rich people feel putting in so much money?

I wonder how they decided how much money to put in?

I wonder why the widow is poor?

I wonder how the poor widow feels giving all she has?

I wonder how she decided to give all she has to live on?

I wonder how Jesus' disciples feel when Jesus says, "This poor widow gave more than all the others"?

Return to the Worship Center Order and continue. The scripture reading is Mark 12:41–44.

MATERIALS

1. Wooden tray
2. Five baskets: one for sitting figures; one for priest and elder; one

for three rich adults, a rich girl, a rich boy; one for the poor widow; and one for coins
3. Sandstone felt Jerusalem underlay* (Use pattern for session 18.)
4. Temple* (use pattern for session 1)
5. Wooden treasury (offering box)
6. Lots of coins (find some from Israel at a coin shop) and two very small copper coins (coin shop may have extremely small ones from Turkey). (**WARNING: Possible choking hazard**. The coins are not suitable for children under three years of age.)
7. Wooden figures:*   ***Sitting***—Jesus, Peter, James, and John
Standing—chief priest, elder, two rich women, a rich man, a rich girl, a rich boy, and the poor widow

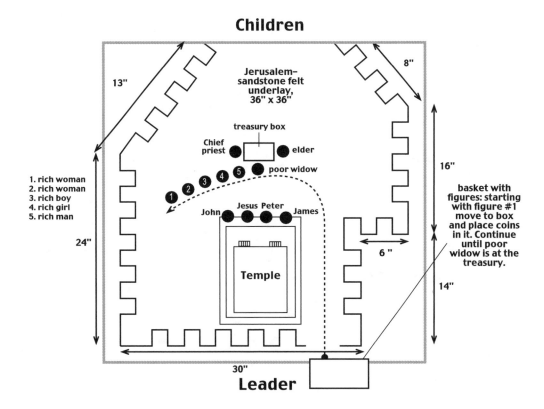

20

A Woman Anoints
Jesus for Burial

Mark 14:3–9; Matthew 26:6–13; John 12:1–8

*Walk slowly to the shelf and pick up the tray with the materials for **A Woman Anoints Jesus for Burial**. Carry it carefully to the circle and set the tray beside you. Take the silver gray felt underlay and lay it out in front of you. Smooth it. Place the backdrop for the house on the underlay at the the center of the edge nearest you. Place the table in the center of the "room," leaving space to place the figures. Place all of the sitting figures around the table except Jesus. Then say:*

Once every year the people of God go up to Jerusalem to celebrate the feast of Passover, to remember how God led them through the waters to freedom. And every year Jesus and his family and friends go up to Jerusalem to celebrate the feast. But this year the chief priests, elders, and scribes were looking for a way to arrest Jesus and have him killed.

Sit back and pause. Then say:

It was two days before Passover, and Jesus was in Simon the leper's house, near Jerusalem.

Present Jesus and place him at the table.

Suddenly a woman appeared with some very expensive ointment.

Present the woman with the flask of ointment and place her near Jesus.

She opened the bottle . . .

Open the bottle.

and poured the ointment over Jesus' head.

Slowly and gently pour it over Jesus' head.

But some became angry. "Why did you waste this ointment? It was very expensive! It could have been sold for a year's wages and the money given to the poor." They kept scolding her. But Jesus said, "Let her alone! She has done a beautiful thing to me. She has anointed my body before I die. She has prepared me to be buried."

Pause. Say firmly:

Then Jesus continued: "Wherever God's story is told around the whole world, what she has done will be told in remembrance of her."

Responding to God's Word:
Wondering Together

I wonder how this woman feels about Jesus?

Touch the woman.

I wonder how Jesus feels about her?

I wonder how the woman feels anointing Jesus?

I wonder why the disciples don't like what the woman is doing for Jesus?

I wonder how the woman feels being scolded?

I wonder why the woman believed Jesus when he said he was going to die and that God would make him alive again?

I wonder why the disciples did not believe this?

I wonder how the woman feels giving away something so precious?

I wonder what this woman is like?

I wonder if she has a name?

I wonder how people who hear this story today feel about this woman?

I wonder how it feels to know someone you love is going to die and you can't do anything about it?

Return to the Worship Center Order and continue. The scripture reading is Mark 14:3–9.

MATERIALS

1. Wooden tray
2. Three baskets: one for Jesus and Simon; one for twelve disciples; one for woman and anointing oil
3. Silver gray felt underlay: 36" by 24"
4. Backdrop for the house* (Same pattern as in session 5.)
5. Round, solid wood table: 6 ¾" in diameter and ¾" thick
6. Round platter: 4" in diameter (make from clay or find in miniature doll house shop)
7. Wooden figures:*   ***Sitting***—Jesus, Simon, and twelve disciples
                        Standing—the woman who anoints Jesus
8. Anointing oil (A small bottle of anointing oil can be purchased at religious bookstores. Or use a sample bottle of sweet-smelling cologne.)

Children

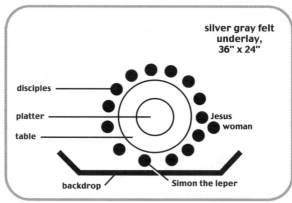

Leader

21

Too Afraid to Follow Jesus
Mark 14; Matthew 26:31–75

Walk slowly to the shelf and pick up the tray with the materials for **Too Afraid to Follow Jesus.** *Carry it carefully to the circle and set the tray beside you. Take the navy blue felt Jerusalem underlay that has the Mount of Olives glued to it and lay it out in front of you. Smooth it and trace the city with your finger as you say:*

This is the city of Jerusalem. So many important things happen in Jerusalem that we need a small piece of it to help us tell the stories. The city is very dark. It must be night. There is a house with a courtyard in the city. Caiaphas, the high priest, lives here.

Place the felt outline of Caiaphas's house on the center-right of the underlay with the door facing the Mount of Olives. (The courtyard is imaginary.) Present and place Caiaphas at the middle of the far 9″ side of the house. Present and place a chief priest to your left of Caiaphas. Present and place an elder to the right of Caiaphas. Present and place a scribe to the left of the chief priest. Place the charcoal fire to the left of the entrance of the house in an imaginary courtyard. Place the servant girl and two bystanders around the fire, leaving room for Peter, later, to stand by the fire near the door.

Outside the city walls is a hill where olive trees grow. It is called the Mount of Olives.

Trace the outline of the Mount of Olives. Place the three trees on it far enough apart that the disciples can move between them. Sit back, pause, and say:

It was night. Jesus was in Jerusalem celebrating the feast of Passover with his disciples.

Present Jesus and hold him in front of you as you continue:

When the feast was over, Jesus said, "Let's go to the Mount of Olives and pray."

Place Jesus facing the trees on the Mount of Olives but far enough away for the eleven disciples to stand between Jesus and the trees. Then place the disciples, except Judas, by the trees, facing Jesus. (Leave the basket you take them from at your left side. You will be placing them in it later, when they run away.)

Then Jesus said to them, "Tonight I will be arrested and you will run away. Later I will be killed. But remember, God will make me alive again. Then I will go ahead of you to Galilee. Meet me there."

Touch Peter's shoulder and say:

But Peter said, "I will always follow you." Jesus replied, "Peter, tonight before the rooster crows, you will deny me three times." Peter insisted, "I will die before I will deny you." Then they saw Judas, one of the twelve disciples, coming with soldiers and a crowd carrying swords and clubs.

Present Judas, and place him near the center of the underlay. Present a soldier and place him beside Judas. Move them to Jesus.

The disciples ran away.

Move the disciples between the trees, and place them in the basket at your left. Hide Peter behind the tree closest to you.

Jesus was arrested and bound.

Wrap a piece of tape around Jesus.

They took Jesus to the house of Caiaphas, the high priest.

Move them to Caiaphas's house.

Peter followed at a distance.

Move Peter, keeping him at a distance from Jesus. Move Judas into the house near the elder. Move Jesus inside, standing opposite Caiaphas. Then move the soldier into the house, standing by the door. Pause. Move Peter to the fire in the courtyard.

They began questioning Jesus about his teaching of the kingdom of God. Jesus said, "Ask those who heard what I taught." One of the soldiers slapped Jesus in the face, and shouted, "Don't talk that way to the high priest."

Now Peter was in the courtyard, keeping warm by a charcoal fire.

Touch Peter's shoulder.

A servant girl said to him,

Touch the servant girl's shoulder.

"You were with Jesus."

"No I wasn't," Peter said.

Then the girl said to the others, "He is one of them."

"No, I'm not!" Peter insisted.

Pause.

And after a while someone else said, "Certainly you are a follower of Jesus."

"I do not know who you are talking about," Peter said. And immediately a rooster crowed. Peter remembered that Jesus had said, "Before the rooster crows you will deny me three times." Peter left.

Move him back to the Mount of Olives and say:

And he cried, and cried, and cried.

Responding to God's Word: Wondering Together

I wonder why Jesus' friends run away when Jesus is in trouble?

I wonder why Judas, who is one of the twelve disciples, would lead the soldiers to arrest Jesus?

I wonder how Jesus feels when he sees his friend Judas?

Move Peter back to the courtyard of Caiaphas's house.

I wonder why Peter says he is not a follower of Jesus?

I wonder how Jesus feels when the people questioning him slap him?

I wonder how the people in the courtyard feel as they listen to what is happening to Jesus?

I wonder why Peter denied Jesus three times?

I wonder what Peter will do when he stops crying?

Move Peter back to the Mount of Olives.

I wonder how Jesus is feeling about being alone and without any friends?

Return to the Worship Center Order and continue. The scripture reading is Matthew 26:31–35.

MATERIALS

1. Wooden tray
2. Six baskets: one for Jesus and eleven disciples; one for felt house outline, Caiaphas, a chief priest, an elder, and a scribe; one for Judas, a soldier, and binding tape; one for a servant girl and two bystanders; one for the charcoal fire; one for three olive trees
3. Navy blue felt for the Jerusalem section of the underlay which will be glued or sewn to the hunter green Mount of Olives felt (See diagram.)
4. Hunter green felt for the Mount of Olives section of the underlay
5. Wooden figures:*   ***Standing***—Jesus, twelve disciples, soldier, Caiaphas, chief priest, elder, scribe, servant girl, and two bystanders
6. Three wooden olive trees*
7. Graystone felt outline for Caiaphas's house*
8. Charcoal fire (Glue small twigs together on a small piece of bark and place dots of red and yellow paint on them for the fire.)
9. Tape for binding Jesus: (⅓″ correction and cover-up tape)

Children

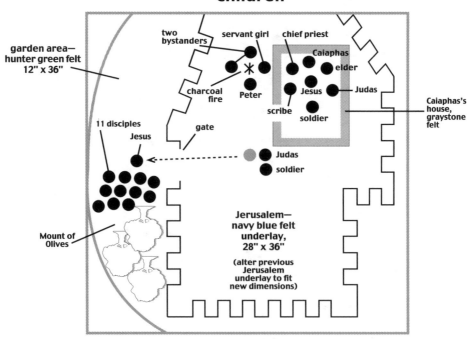

Leader

22

Jesus' Trial

Matthew 27:3–5; Mark 15:1–15; Luke 22:66–71

Walk slowly to the shelf and pick up the tray with the materials for **Jesus' Trial.** *Carry it carefully to the circle and set the tray beside you. Take the sandstone Jerusalem underlay (without the Mount of Olives attached) and lay it out in front of you. Carefully smooth it and trace the outline with your finger as you say:*

> This is the city of Jerusalem. So many important things happen in Jerusalem that we need a small piece of it to help us tell the stories. Caiaphas, the high priest, lives here.

Place the felt outline of Caiaphas's house on the underlay to your center right. Place Caiaphas, a chief priest, an elder, a scribe, and a soldier in the house. Place the Temple near you, to your left, and place a chief priest and elder by the entrance. Sit back, still looking at the underlay, and say:

> It is morning in Jerusalem. Last night Jesus was arrested, taken to the house of Caiaphas, the high priest, and put on trial.

Present Jesus and place him in the house facing Caiaphas.

> Caiaphas, the chief priests, the scribes, and the elders tried to find Jesus guilty so he could be killed. But they couldn't. Finally, Caiaphas asked,

Touch Caiaphas's shoulder.

> "Are you the Christ?" Jesus said, "I am." Caiaphas cried, "You are not the Christ! You are speaking evil against God!" And they all cried, "Jesus should die!"

Point to the people around Caiaphas as you say, "Jesus should die." Pause.

> When morning came, they gathered to plan how to have Jesus killed.

Pause. Present Judas and hold him as you say:

> Judas had been paid thirty pieces of silver to help arrest Jesus.

Place Judas in the center of the underlay. Take the moneybag from the tray and place it beside Judas. Continue:

But when Judas saw they planned to kill Jesus, he was sorry. He went to the chief priests and elders to return the money.

Move Judas to the Temple with your left hand while your right hand is holding the moneybag so it appears that Judas is carrying it. Stop in front of the chief priest and elder.

"I have sinned," Judas said to them. "Jesus is innocent. Don't kill him." But they replied, "What do we care?" And they would not listen to Judas.

Pause, giving Judas time to think. Then say:

Judas threw the money on the floor . . .

Toss the thirty silver coins out of the bag so they scatter in front of the priest and elder.

and left.

Move Judas along the side of the Temple to your left. After he is at the edge of the underlay move him behind you and place him on the tray.

And in great sorrow, Judas hanged himself and died.

Responding to God's Word:
Wondering Together

I wonder how Jesus is feeling while he is on trial?

I wonder why the chief priests, the scribes, and the elders do not believe Jesus is the Christ?

I wonder why they want him dead?

I wonder why they want to kill Jesus just because they do not agree with him?

I wonder how they could have settled their differences besides wanting to hurt or kill?

Place Judas in front of the chief priest and elder at the Temple.

I wonder what it is like for Judas to know that Jesus will be killed?

I wonder how Judas feels when he confesses to the chief priests and elders that he had sinned?

I wonder why the chief priests and elders will not listen to Judas?

I wonder why they will not forgive Judas?

I wonder why when Peter was sorry he denied Jesus, Peter went out and cried and cried, but Judas killed himself?

I wonder what other ways Judas could have handled his guilt and sadness besides killing himself?

I wonder how Judas could have been helped not to kill himself?

I wonder how the disciples feel when they hear that Judas is dead?

Return to the Worship Center Order and continue. The scripture reading is Matthew 27:3–5.

MATERIALS

1. Wooden tray
2. Four baskets: one for Caiaphas, chief priest, elder, scribe, and soldier; one for the chief priest and elder at the Temple; one for Judas and the money bag with thirty silver coins; one for Jesus
3. Sandstone felt Jerusalem underlay (Use pattern from session 18.)
4. Graystone felt outline for Caiaphas's house* (Use pattern from session 21.)
5. Wooden figures:* **Standing**—Jesus, Judas, Caiaphas, two chief priests, two elders, scribe, and a soldier
6. Temple* (Use pattern from session 1.)
7. Thirty silver coins (Purchase small Israeli coins at a coin shop.)
8. Small cloth moneybag for the coins (4″ by 2″ with drawstring)

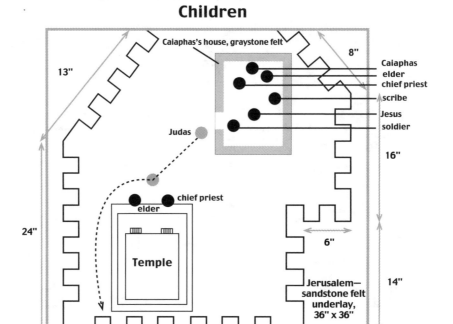

23

Jesus Dies and God Makes Jesus Alive Again

Mark 15

Walk slowly to the shelf and pick up the tray with the materials for **Jesus Dies and God Makes Jesus Alive Again.** *Carry it carefully to the circle and set the tray beside you. Take the Jerusalem underlay that is glued to the apple green felt that represents the place of Jesus' crucifixion and burial and lay it out in front of you. Smooth it, and trace the city walls as you say:*

This is the city of Jerusalem. So many important things happen in Jerusalem that we need a small piece of it to help us tell the stories. This is the head-quarters of Pilate, the governor.

Place the backdrop for Pilate's headquarters near the back edge of the under-lay closest to you, to your far left. Place Pilate at the center back of the back-drop. Place a guard, elder, chief priest, and scribe in a semicircle facing Pilate. (The guard should be to your left of the others so you can move the guard with your left hand to Jesus and move Jesus with your right when taking both away later.)

Outside the city walls is a place for burial.

Place the tomb at the back edge of the green part of the underlay at your right. Place the stone along the wall by the entrance. Sit back, pause, then say:

Once every year Jesus went up to Jerusalem to celebrate the feast of Passover.

Present Jesus and hold him in front of you and continue:

But this Passover Jesus was arrested and put on trial because some people wanted to put Jesus to death. But only the government could put someone to death. So they took Jesus to Pilate, the governor, and a great crowd watched.

Place Jesus facing Pilate and motion with your hand to represent a great crowd.

Pilate questioned Jesus. "I find no reason to kill this man," he said.

But the crowd shouted, "No! Kill him! Crucify him!" They continued shouting until, finally, Pilate agreed.

So they took Jesus outside the city wall to be crucified.

Move the guard to Jesus and then move both to the place of crucifixion. When you say the following, present and move each woman so she faces Jesus and the spot where the cross will be placed.

Now some disciples of Jesus were not afraid to follow him. Mary Magdalene, . . . Mary, the mother of James and Joses, . . . Salome, . . . Mary the mother of Jesus, . . . and many other women disciples followed Jesus to the place where Jesus would be crucified.

Make a slow hand motion to represent the other women.

At nine o'clock in the morning Jesus' hands and feet were nailed to the cross.

Take the cross and place Jesus on it. Stand it up beside the guard.

At noon, darkness covered the whole land.

Stretch your arms straight out from your sides and move them forward in a circular motion until your hands touch and your arms encircle the area. Keeping your arms in a circular position, lower them, to portray darkness covering the land, and pause. Sit back and pause.

At three o'clock Jesus died.

Pause.

And the curtain of the Temple was torn in two, from top to bottom. The guard said, "This man really is the Christ."

Pause.

Then Joseph of Arimathea,

Present Joseph and place him facing Jesus on the cross.

who longed for the kingdom of God, took Jesus' body,

Lower the cross and remove Jesus' body.

and wrapped it in a linen cloth.

Wrap it in a linen cloth (See session 16 for instructions for wrapping the body.)

Joseph of Arimathea went to his own tomb and placed Jesus' body in it.

Move them to the tomb and place Jesus inside.

He rolled a stone against the door.

Roll the stone in front of the door.

Mary Magdalene and Mary the mother of James and Joses saw where Jesus' body was laid.

Move them near the tomb. Sit quietly for a moment.

Responding to God's Word:
Wondering Together

I wonder how Joseph of Arimathea feels placing Jesus in his tomb?

I wonder how Mary Magdalene feels seeing her best friend die?

Gently touch her shoulder.

I wonder how Mary, the mother of James and Joses, feels?

Gently touch her shoulder.

Move the two Marys back to the other women.

I wonder how Jesus' mother feels?

I wonder how Salome feels?

I wonder how the people feel when darkness covers the whole earth?

I wonder how the people feel when they hear the guard say, "This really is the Christ"?

Now listen carefully. I have some very good news. On Sunday, the third day after Jesus died, God made Jesus alive again. God raised Jesus from the dead, just as Jesus said God would do.

PLEASE NOTE: *Always tell of Jesus' resurrection when you tell of the crucifixion. Be prepared for sadness and disbelief that Jesus died. Be sure everyone hears that God Made Jesus Alive Again.*

Return to the Worship Center Order and continue. The scripture reading is Mark 15:33–41.

MATERIALS

1. Wooden tray
2. Three baskets: one for Pilate, guard, elder, chief priest, and scribe; one for Jesus, Joseph of Arimathea, and the linen cloth; one for the four women.
3. Sandstone felt Jerusalem underlay with apple green felt garden area for the crucifixion and tomb attached to the Jerusalem underlay at your right
4. Backdrop for Pilate's headquarters* (Use pattern from session 11.)
5. Wooden platform with cross*
6. Wooden figures:* **Standing**—Jesus, Jesus (with outstreched hands), Pilate, guard (soldier), elder, chief priest, scribe, Mary Magdalene, Mary the mother of James and Joses, Salome, Mary the mother of Jesus, and Joseph of Arimathea
7. Tomb* with stone
8. White square linen cloth to place over Jesus' face: 4″ by 4″.
9. White linen cloth to wrap Jesus' body: 16″ long by 6″ wide. (Fold it every 2″ so you can unfold it to wrap Jesus. See session 16 for wrapping directions.)

Children

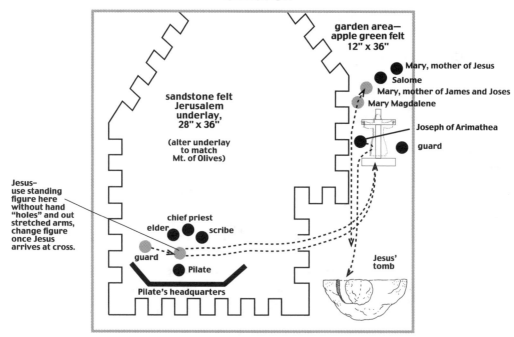

Leader

24

Jesus Appears to Mary Magdalene

Mark 16:1–11

Walk slowly to the shelf and pick up the tray with the materials for **Jesus Appears to Mary Magdalene.** *Carry it carefully to the circle and place it beside you. Sit quietly while you feel the story forming in you. Then place the white felt circular underlay in front of you and smooth it as you say:*

This is the story of Easter, the time we celebrate the mystery that Jesus died and that God made Jesus alive again.

Roll out the road. Place the tomb at the end of the road near you. Place the stone beside the door so the tomb is open. Then say:

This is a tomb, a special place for the dead.

Gently run your hand over the tomb.

When Jesus died, Joseph of Arimathea put Jesus' body in his tomb and rolled a huge stone in front of the door.

Trace the stone, which is beside the door of the tomb.

Very early, on Sunday morning, Mary Magdalene,

Present Mary Magdalene and place her on the road. Present and place the remaining women behind Mary Magdalene on the road after you say their names.

and Mary the mother of James . . . and Salome . . . went to the tomb with spices to anoint Jesus' body.

Begin moving them toward the tomb.

"Who will roll away the stone for us?" they wondered.

When they are near the tomb, stop and say:

But when they looked up, the tomb was open. They went in.

Move them into the tomb.

Jesus was gone! Then they saw a young man wearing a white robe. He said, "Don't be afraid. Jesus is alive. Go tell the disciples and Peter that Jesus is going ahead of you to Galilee, just as he said. Meet him there." They were amazed and fled from the tomb.

Move Salome and Mary the mother of James swiftly down the road, with Mary Magdalene following. Stop them near the end of the road and say:

They were afraid to tell anyone.

Then turn Mary Magdalene and move her back toward the tomb, to about the center of the road, and say:

Now an amazing thing had happened. God had raised Jesus from the dead.

Present Jesus and hold him while you say:

God had made Jesus alive again.

Place Jesus on the road beside Mary and say:

And the very first person Jesus appeared to was Mary Magdalene.

Pause, giving them time to "talk." Look at Mary Magdalene and say:

Now Mary Magdalene was no longer afraid. She went to Jesus' friends,

Move Mary Magdalene back to Mary and Salome, pause, then turn her toward your left and move her off of the road to the center edge of the underlay, and say:

and said, "Jesus is alive. I saw him. Meet him in Galilee, just as he said."

Pause:

But they did not believe her.

**Responding to God's Word:
Wondering Together**

I wonder how Mary Magdalene feels when the person she loves the most dies?

Move Mary toward the tomb. Place other figures on the underlay as you ask questions about them.

I wonder how Mary Magdalene feels going to Jesus' tomb?

I wonder how the women feel when they do not see Jesus' body in the tomb?

I wonder why they are too afraid to tell that Jesus is alive?

I wonder how Mary Magdalene feels when Jesus appears to her?

I wonder why Jesus appears to Mary Magdalene first?

I wonder why Mary Magdalene is no longer afraid to tell Jesus' friends that Jesus is alive?

I wonder why they do not believe Mary Magdalene when she tells them Jesus is alive?

I wonder how she feels when they do not believe her?

I wonder what she will do?

Return to the Worship Center Order and continue. The scripture reading is Mark 16:1–11.

MATERIALS

1. Wooden tray
2. Two baskets: one for the three women; one for the young man and Jesus
3. White felt circular underlay: 36″ in diameter
4. Cashmere tan felt road to tomb: 30″ long by 5″ wide, curved (See diagram.)
5. Tomb* and large round stone (See pattern for session 23.)
6. Wooden figures:*   **Standing**—Mary Magdalene, Mary the mother of James, Salome, young man, and Jesus (with nail marks)

Children

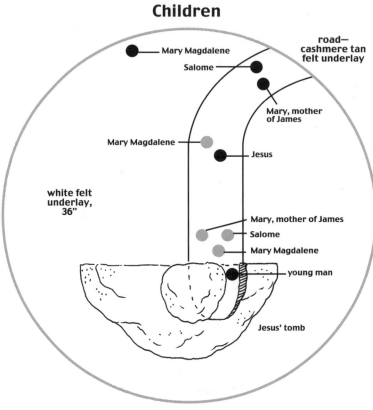

Mary Magdalene

Salome

road—
cashmere tan
felt underlay

Mary, mother
of James

Mary Magdalene

Jesus

white felt
underlay,
36"

Mary, mother of James

Salome

Mary Magdalene

young man

Jesus' tomb

Leader

25

Jesus Appears to Thomas

John 20:19–29

Walk slowly to the shelf and pick up the tray with the materials for **Jesus Appears to Thomas.** *Carry it carefully to the circle and set the tray beside you. Take the pirate green felt underlay and lay it out in front of you. Smooth it as you say:*

> After God raised Jesus from the dead, Jesus' disciples continued to meet on Sunday, the first day of the week.

Place the wooden backdrop and table on the underlay at the center of the edge nearest you. Place the disciples around the table except for Thomas. Then say:

> This Sunday the disciples were happy because last week they had seen Jesus, alive, in this very room. Jesus had said to them, "Peace be with you. As God has *sent* me, so I *send* you to do what I have said and done." Then Jesus breathed on them and said, "Receive the Holy Spirit."

Pause and present Thomas, holding him as you say:

> But Thomas had not been with them. Thomas said, "Unless I see and touch the nail marks in his hands and touch his side, I will not believe Jesus is alive."

Place Thomas at the center of the table on the side farthest from you.

> They closed the doors.

Close the doors.

> But suddenly someone appeared.

Present Jesus and place him near Thomas. Turn Thomas to face Jesus.

> "Peace be with you," he said. Then he said, "Thomas, look at my hands. . . . Come and touch them. . . . And put your hand in my side. Stop doubting and believe."
> Thomas said, "My Lord and my God."

"Thomas," Jesus said, "do you believe because you see me? Blessed is everyone who has not seen me and yet they believe."

Responding to God's Word:
Wondering Together

I wonder why Thomas doesn't believe the disciples when they say, "Jesus is alive"?

I wonder how the disciples feel when Thomas will not believe them?

I wonder how Thomas feels seeing Jesus alive?

I wonder why Thomas calls Jesus "My Lord and my God"?

I wonder how people who have not seen Jesus believe that God raised Jesus from the dead?

I wonder how the disciples feel as Jesus breathes on them and says, "Receive the Holy Spirit"?

I wonder how they feel when they receive the Holy Spirit?

I wonder how the disciples feel when Jesus says: "As God has sent me into the world, so I send you to do what I have said and done"?

I wonder what Mary Magdalene will do as Jesus sends her?

I wonder what Peter will do?

I wonder what the other disciples will do?

Return to the Worship Center Order and continue. The scripture reading is John 20:19–29.

MATERIALS

1. Wooden tray
2. Two baskets: one for Jesus and Thomas; one for the rest of the figures
3. Pirate green felt underlay: 36″ by 24″
4. Table:* 8½″ by 3″
5. Backdrop with doors*

6. Wooden figures:*   **Standing**—Thomas, Peter, Andrew, James, John, Mary Magdalene, Mary the mother of Jesus, Salome, Mary the mother of James and Joses, Joanna, girl, boy, and Jesus (with nail marks)

Children

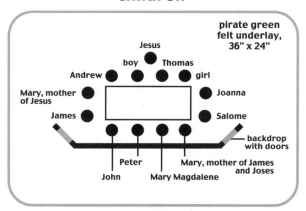

Leader

26

Jesus Commissions the Disciples
Matthew 28:16–20; Mark 16:15–18

*Walk slowly to the shelf and pick up the tray with the materials for **Jesus Commissions the Disciples**. Carry it carefully to the circle and set the tray beside you. Take the green and blue felt Galilean underlay and lay it out in front of you, with the green closest to you. Smooth it, and point to the place where the green and blue meet at your right and say:*

This is the Sea of Galilee.

Trace the sea all around its edge, moving counterclockwise. Then say:

So many important things happen by the sea that we need a small piece of it to help us tell the stories.

Move your hands over the sea, portraying the following actions, with your voice full of wonder and amazement, and then with calmness as you end.

The sea is a wonderful and strange place. . . . When the wind blows . . . the sea becomes very rough and wild. And when the wind is calm . . . the sea is peaceful and still.

Pause and enjoy the calm. Then present the mountain and place it at the center of the green part of the underlay at the edge near you. Place Jesus on the mountain. Pause and sit back a moment. Then say:

After God raised Jesus from the dead, the eleven disciples returned to this mountain in Galilee, just as Jesus told them to do.

Take John and Peter from the tray and move them up the side of the mountain to your right, onto the ledge just below Jesus. They should face Jesus, with Peter opposite Jesus. Then move James up the mountain to stand beside Peter. Move Andrew and Philip up your right side of the mountain and onto the next ledge as far as they can go to your left. They should face Jesus. Move the remaining disciples up the mountain by twos until all are on the next ledge and facing Jesus in this order: Bartholomew and Levi; Thomas and James; and Thaddaeus and Simon.

When they saw Jesus, they worshiped him; but some doubted.

Pause. Then say:

Then Jesus said, "I am *sending* you to the whole world to do what I have done and to show every one the way of the kingdom of God. I am *commissioning* you to do this."
Then Jesus said these special words to them: "All authority in heaven and on earth has been given to me. Go therefore and make disciples of all nations, baptizing them in the name of the Father and of the Son and of the Holy Spirit, and teaching them to obey everything that I have commanded you. And remember, I am with you always, to the end of the age."

Pause.

And when the disciples received the Holy Spirit, they were filled with so much love that they did what Jesus asked them to do.

Beginning with the two disciples at your right on the lower ledge, move them down your right side of the mountain and on the underlay to your right. (You will be forming a semicircle of disciples below the mountain.)

They cast out unclean spirits.

Move the next two disciples down the mountain to your middle right on the underlay.

They healed the sick.

Beginning with the two disciples at your left on the lower ledge, move them down your left side of the mountain and on the underlay to your left.

They encouraged the poor.

Move the next two disciples down the mountain to your middle left.

And they enjoyed the children.

Place your right hand on James and your left on John and move them simultaneously down the right and left side of the mountain toward the front of the underlay. Then move Peter down the right side of the mountain to center front, completing the semicircle. Peter will be opposite Jesus, who remains on the mountain. Then say:

They did this in Jerusalem, in Judea, in Samaria, and in all the nations, showing the way of the kingdom of God and baptizing everyone who would follow Jesus.

Responding to God's Word:
Wondering Together

I wonder why some believe this person is Jesus and others doubt?

Touch Jesus' arm.

I wonder how the ones who believe know that this is Jesus?

I wonder how they feel being close to Jesus?

I wonder how they feel as Jesus commissions them and sends them out to show the way of the kingdom of God?

I wonder what each one will do to show the way of the kingdom of God?

I wonder what they will tell about Jesus?

I wonder how they feel to have Jesus with them always, even when they can't see Jesus?

I wonder how they know Jesus is with them?

I wonder who they think Jesus really is?

I wonder if they will always follow Jesus even if they can't see him?

I wonder how they feel when they hear Jesus say, "And remember, I am with you always, to the end of the age"?

These words that Jesus said when he sent out his disciples are so important they have a name.

Present the card with the great commission written on it. Move your hand across the words THE GREAT COMMISSION *at the top of the card.*

They are called "The Great Commission." The Great Commission is for us too. These words are so important that the church still says them to those who will follow Jesus and do the special things to show the way of the kingdom of God.

Stand the card on the underlay between the mountain and the disciples.

> *Return to the Worship Center Order and continue. The scripture reading is Matthew 28:16–20.*

MATERIALS

1. Wooden tray
2. Two baskets for figures, one for Jesus and one for the eleven disciples
3. Lime green and blueberry bash felt underlay (Use pattern in session 2.)
4. Mountain* (Use pattern in session 6.)
5. Wooden figures:*   ***Standing***—Jesus (with outstretched hands), eleven disciples (Judas is dead)
6. Card* with the Great Commission written on it (mount and laminate)

Children

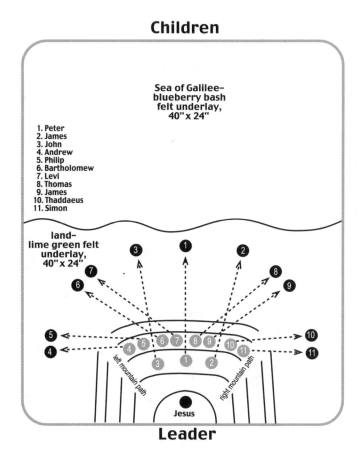

Leader

27

Jesus Appears to the Disciples by the Sea

John 21:1–13

Walk slowly to the shelf and pick up the tray with the materials for **Jesus Appears to the Disciples by the Sea.** *Carry it carefully to the circle and set the tray beside you. Take the green and blue felt underlay and lay it out in front of you. Gently smooth it. Then point to the place where the green and blue meet at your right and say:*

This is the Sea of Galilee.

Trace the sea all around its edge, moving counterclockwise. Then say:

So many important things happen by the sea that we need a small piece of it to help us tell the stories.

Move your hand over the sea, portraying the following actions, with your voice full of wonder and amazement, and then with calmness as you end.

The sea is a wonderful and strange place. . . . When the wind blows . . . the sea becomes very rough and wild. And when the wind is calm . . . the sea is peaceful and still.

Pause and enjoy the calm. Then place the boat by the shore near the left edge of the underlay and say:

After God raised Jesus from the dead, Jesus' disciples returned to Galilee, where Jesus told them to meet him. One evening seven of them decided to go fishing.

Place Peter, Thomas, Bartholomew (Nathanael), James, and John and two others (Philip and Andrew) in the boat. Push the boat out into the water. Toss the net over the left (port) side of the boat. Pull it in empty, and toss it out again a few times. Move the boat to several fishing spots and finally turn it so the bow (front) of the boat is headed toward shore. Toss the net to the left (port) side, wait, and say:

They fished all night but caught nothing. Just after daybreak, they saw someone on the beach.

Present Jesus and place him to your left of center on the beach, looking at the disciples, leaving space for the charcoal fire and disciples to stand, later, on the land.

But they couldn't tell who it was. He called to them, "Have you caught any fish?"

"No," they answered.

"Cast the net to the right side of the boat, and you will find some." So they did.

Cast the net from the right (starboard) side of the boat. Keeping your eye on the net, fill it with wooden fish from the basket on the tray.

Now there were so many fish they couldn't pull in the net.

Try, unsuccessfully, to pull in the net. Then say:

Someone said, "It's Jesus!" Peter jumped into the water and ran to him.

Move Peter through the water to Jesus' right.

The others came in the boat, dragging the net.

Move the boat and net to the shore, to the right of Jesus.

When they came ashore, they saw a charcoal fire . . .

Place the charcoal fire on the shore.

with fish and bread on it. "Come and eat," Jesus said.

Move the disciples into a circle around Jesus and say:

The disciples realized this was Jesus. Then Jesus took the bread and gave it to them . . .

Pass imaginary bread to each disciple.

and also the fish.

Pass imaginary fish to each.

Responding to God's Word:
Wondering Together

I wonder how the disciples feel when Jesus doesn't seem to be around anymore?

I wonder why they decide to go fishing?

I wonder what they are talking about while they are fishing?

I wonder how they feel, fishing all night and catching nothing?

I wonder how the person on the beach knows where the fish are?

I wonder how the disciples know the person on the beach is Jesus?

I wonder what Jesus and the disciples are saying to each other?

I wonder what they will do now that they have talked with Jesus again?

Return to the Worship Center Order and continue. The scripture reading is John 21:1–13.

MATERIALS

1. Wooden tray
2. Four baskets: one for Jesus; one for the seven disciples; one for the charcoal fire; one for the fish
3. Lime green and blueberry bash felt underlay (Use pattern in session 2.)
4. Wooden figures:*   **Standing**—Jesus (with nail marks), Peter, Thomas, Bartholomew (Nathanael), James, John, Philip, and Andrew
5. Boat* (See pattern from session 2.)
6. Fishnet (See directions for session 2.)
7. Wooden fish*
8. Charcoal fire (See directions for session 21.)

Children

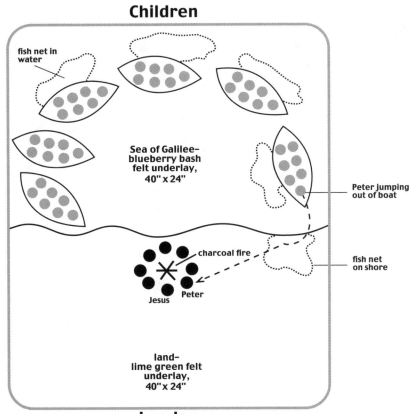

Leader

28

Jesus Again Asks
Peter to Follow Him

John 21:15–17 and 21:19b

Walk slowly to the shelf and pick up the tray with the materials for **Jesus Again Asks Peter to Follow Him.** *Carry it carefully to the circle and set the tray beside you. Take the green and blue felt underlay and lay it out in front of you. Smooth it. Then point to the place where the green and blue meet at your right and say:*

This is the Sea of Galilee.

Trace the sea all around its edge, moving counterclockwise. Then say:

So many important things happen by the sea that we need a small piece of it to help us tell the stories.

Move your hand over the sea, portraying the following actions, filling your voice with wonder and amazement, and then with calmness as you end.

The sea is a wonderful and strange place. . . . When the wind blows . . . the sea becomes very rough and wild. And when the wind is calm . . . the sea is peaceful and still.

Pause and enjoy the calm. Then place the boat by the shore near the left edge of the underlay and say:

After God raised Jesus from the dead, Jesus' disciples returned to Galilee, where Jesus told them to meet him. One evening seven of them decided to go fishing.

Place Peter, Thomas, Bartholomew (Nathanael), James, John, and two others (Philip and Andrew) in the boat. Push the boat out into the water. Toss the net over the left (port) side of the boat. Pull it in empty and toss it out again several times. Move the boat to several fishing spots and finally turn it so the bow (front) of the boat is headed toward shore. Toss the net to the port side, wait, and say:

They fished all night but caught nothing. Just after daybreak, they saw some-one on the beach.

Present Jesus, and place him to your left of center on the beach, looking at the disciples, leaving space for the charcoal fire and disciples to stand, later, on the land.

But they couldn't tell who it was. He called to them, "Have you caught any fish?"

"No," they answered.

"Cast the net to the right side of the boat, and you will find some." So they did.

Cast the net from the right (starboard) side of the boat. Keeping your eye on the net, fill it with wooden fish from the basket on the tray.

Now there were so many fish they couldn't pull in the net.

Try, unsuccessfully, to pull in the net. Then say:

Someone said, "It's Jesus!" Peter jumped into the water and ran to him.

Move Peter through the water to Jesus' right.

The others came in the boat, dragging the net.

Move the boat and net to the shore, to the right of Jesus.

When they came ashore, they saw a charcoal fire . . .

Place the charcoal fire on the shore, and continue:

with fish and bread on it. "Come and eat," Jesus said.

Move the disciples into a circle around Jesus and say:

The disciples realized this was Jesus. Then Jesus took the bread and gave it to them . . .

Pass imaginary bread to each disciple.

and also the fish.

Pass imaginary fish to each disciple. Pause for eating. Then turn Jesus toward Peter and say:

When they had finished eating, Jesus said to Peter, "Peter do you love me more than these?"

"Yes," Peter answered, "you know that I love you."

Jesus said, "Feed my lambs."
A second time Jesus asked, "Peter do you love me?"
Peter said, "Yes, you know I love you."
Jesus said, "Tend my sheep."
A third time Jesus asked, "Peter do you love me?"
Peter was very sad because Jesus asked him a third time. Peter replied, "You know everything; you know that I love you." Jesus said to Peter, "Feed my sheep."

Pause. Then say:

Then Jesus said, "Peter, *follow me.*"

Move Jesus to your left edge of the underlay, with Peter walking along with Jesus.

Responding to God's Word: Wondering Together

I wonder how Peter feels being with Jesus?

I wonder how Peter feels when Jesus asks, "Do you love me more than these"?

I wonder how Peter feels when Jesus said, "Feed my sheep"?

I wonder how Peter feels following Jesus now?

I wonder where Jesus is leading him?

I wonder what kind of "shepherd" Peter will be?

Return to the Worship Center Order and continue. The scripture reading is John 21:15–17; 19b.

MATERIALS

1. Wooden tray
2. Four baskets: one for Jesus; one for the seven disciples; one for the charcoal fire; one for the wooden fish
3. Lime green and blueberry bash felt underlay (See directions for session 2.)
4. Wooden figures:* **Standing**—Jesus (with nail marks), Peter, Thomas, Bartholomew (Nathanael), James, John, Philip, and Andrew

5. Boat* (Use pattern from session 2.)
6. Fishnet (See directions for session 2.)
7. Wooden fish* (See pattern for session 27.)
8. Charcoal fire (See directions for session 21.)

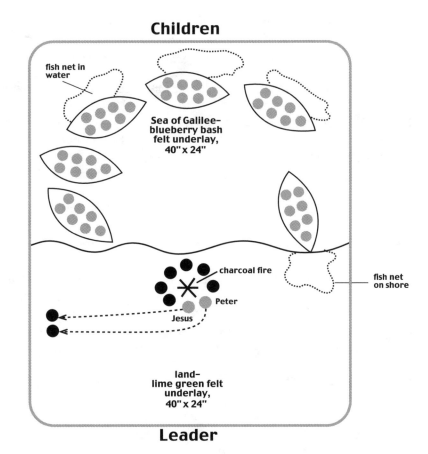

29

God's Gift of the Holy Spirit
Isaiah 11:2–3a and Acts 1:3–5; 1:8

Walk slowly to the shelf and pick up the tray with the materials for **God's Gift of the Holy Spirit.*** *Carry it carefully to the circle and set the tray beside you. Take the white underlay and lay it out in front of you. Smooth it and say:*

One day, after God made Jesus alive again, Jesus said to his disciples, "God is going to give you a special gift—the gift of the Holy Spirit—so you can do what I have done and say what I have said. You will not see me any longer. But remember, I will be with you always. I will be with you in every time and every place." Then Jesus ascended to God.
Later God gave the disciples the gift of the Holy Spirit.

Place the red, seven-tongued flame on the white underlay.

When they received the gift of the Holy Spirit, they received seven gifts.

Place the seven felt flames on the red underlay. Start with an orange flame. The wider end goes to the point at the base of the red underlay. The sharper pointed end goes to the top of the flame. Place a gold flame next. Continue alternating the orange and gold flames. After the first four are placed, turn the remaining flames over so they will fit the direction of the underlay. Pause, and then say:

They received the gift of the spirit of wisdom.

Present a card with the words "Spirit of Wisdom" written on it. Place it on the felt flame farthest to your right. Then place a white candle above the point of the felt flame. Light the candle and say:

Let's enjoy God's gift of the spirit of wisdom.

Pause awhile to enjoy the gift. Then say:

*****WARNING**! **Possible fire hazard**. Possible burning hazards from wax falling on skin. Do not leave candles unattended or allow children to use this material without an adult. Do not use candles if it is against your city's fire code, or for any reason you do not wish to use them. *Do not allow children to light or extinguish these candles.* Take all matches from the room when you leave.

They received the spirit of understanding.

Present a card with the words "Spirit of Understanding" written on it. Place it on the next felt flame. Then place a white candle above the point of the felt flame. Light the candle and say:

Let's enjoy the gift of the spirit of understanding.

Pause to enjoy the gift. Repeat this procedure for the next five gifts. Say the name of the gift, present the card, place it on the felt flame, place a white candle above the point of the felt flame, light the candle and pause to enjoy the gift.

They received the spirit of counsel.

Repeat above procedure.

Let's enjoy the gift of the spirit of counsel.

Pause.

They received the spirit of might.

Repeat above procedure.

Let's enjoy the gift of the spirit of might.

Pause.

They received the spirit of knowledge.

Repeat above procedure.

Let's enjoy the gift of the spirit of knowledge.

Pause.

They received the spirit of awe of God.

Repeat above procedure.

Let's enjoy the gift of the spirit of awe of God.

Pause.

They received the spirit of joy in the presence of God.

Repeat above procedure.

Let's enjoy the gift of the spirit of joy in the presence of God.

Pause.

When the disciples received the Holy Spirit and these wonderful gifts of the Spirit, they were filled with so much love that they began telling about Jesus and showing the way of the kingdom of God. They did this in Jerusalem, in Judea, in Samaria, and throughout the whole world.

Responding to God's Word:
Wondering Together

I wonder how the disciples feel when they receive these gifts of the Holy Spirit?

I wonder how the other followers of Jesus feel when they receive the gift of the Holy Spirit and the gifts the Holy Spirit gives them?

I wonder how Jesus' followers feel when they receive the gift of the spirit of wisdom?

I wonder what they will do with the gift of the spirit of wisdom?

Wonder about each of the gifts. When you are finished wondering say:

These gifts of the Holy Spirit are still given to those who follow Jesus and are baptized and receive God's gift of the Holy Spirit. They help us love God, follow Jesus, and show the way of the kingdom of God.

Now these gifts don't stay in this room. They are with us wherever we are. Let's change the candles to help us remember that God's gifts are with us always, in every time and every place.

The spirit of wisdom . . .

Snuff out the flames as you name the gift each represents.

and understanding, . . .
the spirit of counsel . . . and might, . . .
the spirit of knowledge . . . and awe of God, . . .
the spirit of joy in the presence of God . . . can be with us always in every time and every place.

NOTE: *If children want to use these materials during the personal response time, you must be with them. Let the children place the felt materials and the cards on the underlay but* **you should sit behind the candles and light them. Do not allow children to light or extinguish these candles.**

> *Return to the Worship Center Order and continue. The scripture reading is Isaiah 11:2–3a; Acts 1:3–5; 1:8.*

LEADERSHIP HINT: *Remember that these gifts are gifts of God. God gives them to us when we receive the Holy Spirit. We cannot choose which ones we want. When it comes to gifts from God, we receive them with gratitude and use them. In many of the liturgies for baptism or confirmation, at the time of the laying on of hands, the minister or priest prays that the Holy Spirit will give these gifts to the persons being baptized or confirmed.*

MATERIALS

1. Wooden tray
2. Three baskets for materials: one for candles; one for candle-holders and snuffer; one for cards
3. Round white felt underlay: 36″ in diameter
4. Red felt for seven-tongued flame underlay*
5. Four orange felt flames*
6. Three gold felt flames*
7. Seven cards,* each with the name of a gift on it
8. Seven 6″ or 8″ white candles, depending on the height of the candle holders
9. Seven low brass candle holders
10. Covered brass or glass container to place burned matches in
11. Matches
12. Candle snuffer

Children

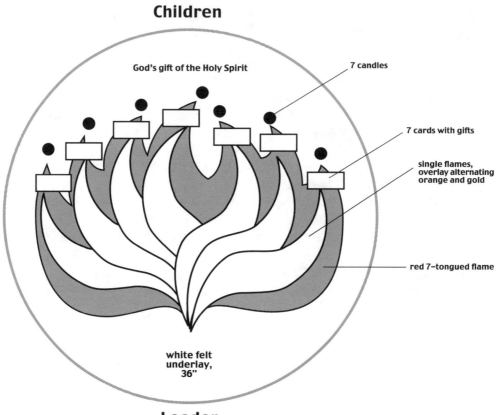

God's gift of the Holy Spirit

7 candles

7 cards with gifts

single flames,
overlay alternating
orange and gold

red 7-tongued flame

white felt
underlay,
36"

Leader

30

Peter, Follower of Jesus,
Heals a Lame Man in Jerusalem

Acts 3:1–16

Walk slowly to the shelf and pick up the tray with the materials for **Peter Heals a Lame Man.** *Carry it carefully to the circle and set the tray beside you. Take out the Jerusalem underlay and lay it in front of you. Smooth it as you say:*

This is the city of Jerusalem. So many important things happen in Jerusalem that we need a small piece of it to help us tell the stories.

Sit back and pause. Then say:

After Jesus went away, so he could be with us always, in every time and every place, Jesus' followers received God's gift of the Holy Spirit. The Holy Spirit gave them so much love that they would do what Jesus would do. They said the wonderful things that Jesus said, and they did the amazing things that Jesus did. They did this first in Jerusalem.

Place the Temple at the center near the edge of the underlay that is closest to you and say:

Now Peter and John were going up to the Temple to pray.

Present Peter and John. Then move them from your lower right corner toward the Temple. Stop them near the Temple and say:

A man who had never been able to walk was being carried to the gate of the Temple.

Present the man lying down on your left hand with your right hand underneath, supporting your left hand. Move your hands, with the man, toward the Temple. Stop and place him on the underlay near the Temple.

He sat there everyday and begged.

Move Peter and John toward the Temple, and when they get to the lame man say:

The man called out, "Money. Money."

Stop Peter and John.

Peter and John looked at him. "Look at us," they said. And he looked. Peter said, "I don't have any money, but I will give you what I have. In the name of Jesus the Christ, stand up and walk." He got up.

Stand the man up.

He began walking . . . and leaping and praising God.

Walk and leap the man around and move him toward the Temple.

And he entered the Temple with Peter and John, still praising God.

Move them to the Temple entrance and say:

The people were filled with wonder and amazement. Then Peter said to them, "We did not heal this man. He was healed by the name of Jesus the Christ, whom you crucified, the one God raised from the dead. By Jesus this man is standing here well. Repent, change the ways you live, and follow the way of the kingdom of God." And about five thousand people did.

Responding to God's Word: Wondering Together

I wonder how the man feels begging for money?

I wonder why the man wouldn't look at Peter and John when he asked them for money?

I wonder how the man feels about Peter and John?

I wonder how the man feels about Jesus the Christ?

I wonder what the man will do now that he can walk?

I wonder how the people feel about what Peter said to them?

I wonder how they will change the way they live?

I wonder what it's like to follow the way of the kingdom of God?

I wonder how they feel when they remember that Jesus was crucified?

I wonder how they feel when they hear that God made Jesus alive again?

I wonder what they will tell others about Jesus and the kingdom of God?

Return to the Worship Center Order and continue. The scripture reading is Acts 3:1–10.

MATERIALS

1. Wooden tray
2. Basket for figures
3. Sandstone felt Jerusalem underlay* (Use pattern from session 18.)
4. Temple* (Use pattern for session 1.)
5. Wooden figures:* **Standing**—Peter, John, and lame man

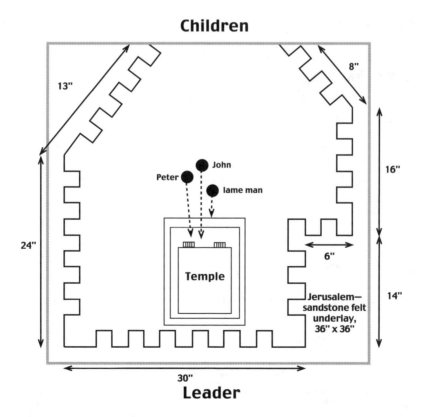

31

Philip, Follower of Jesus, Teaches in Samaria

Acts 8:4–25

Walk slowly to the shelf and pick up the tray with the materials for **Philip, Follower of Jesus, Goes to Samaria.** *Carry it carefully to the circle and set the tray beside you. Take the cashmere tan underlay and lay it out in front of you. Smooth it. Roll out the denim felt stream to your left and then place the city wall so the left edge of it touches the stream. Then say:*

This is part of the land of Samaria. So many important things happen in Samaria that we need a small piece of it to help us tell the stories.

Sit back and pause:

When the gift of the Holy Spirit was given to Jesus' followers, they were filled with so much love that amazing things happened. They did what Jesus would do. Peter and John did this first in Jerusalem, and Philip went to a city in Samaria.

Present Philip and place him at the center in front of the city wall.

Crowds of people came to listen to Philip teach about Jesus the Christ and the kingdom of God.

Present and place a man to the right of Philip.

Some had unclean spirits.

Present and place a woman beside the man.

Some were paralyzed.

Present and place the paralyzed person opposite the woman with the unclean spirit so that a space is left opposite of Philip where Simon the magician will be placed later. (The people will form a circle around Philip. But leave enough room for Peter and John to move to Philip later and to stand in front of the two people on either side.)

Some were lame.

Place a lame child by the paralyzed person.

Now as Philip was teaching about the kingdom of God, unclean spirits suddenly started screaming and coming out of many people.

Toss the woman with the unclean spirit and then stand her still again.

The paralyzed began to walk.

Stand up the paralyzed person, walk her around a little, and return her to the circle.

The lame were healed.

Take the crutch from the child and walk him around.

Everyone was joyful.

Move your hand in a circle above their heads. Then pause.

Now there was a man in this city who did magic.

Present Simon and hold him while you say:

His name was Simon. The people called him the "Great Power." They followed him because he could do magic.

Place Simon opposite Philip.

Now as Philip was telling them about Jesus and the kingdom of God, they began saying, "We want to follow Jesus."
So Philip baptized them.

Move Philip to the stream. Then move the man who was standing to the right of Philip to the stream and place him under the water in the pocket in the felt stream. Cup your hand over his head. Then return him to his place in the circle. Move the next person to the stream and repeat the action. Skip Simon, who will be baptized last. Baptize the other two persons. Then say:

Even Simon the magician believed and was baptized.

Baptize Simon and return him to his place. Move Philip back to his place. Then sit back and pause a moment.

Now the people were baptized, but they had not received the Holy Spirit. So Peter and John came from Jerusalem.

Present Peter and John. Move them from your right and into the circle, with each one facing the two people on either side of Philip.

Peter and John began praying.

Pause.

Then they laid their hands on the people.

Put the thumb and index finger together of each of your hands and touch the foreheads of the people on each side of Philip. (The index finger will touch the edge of the head and the thumb will touch the forehead.) Then say:

And they received the Holy Spirit.

Repeat for the foreheads of the next two people and then Simon. (Remember that Philip has already received the Holy Spirit at Pentecost.) Pause and move Peter and John to Philip. Place Peter to Philip's right and John to Philip's left, facing the people. Pause, and then say:

Now when Simon saw that the Holy Spirit was given through the laying on of Peter's and John's hands, Simon took some money . . .

Put the money, from the basket on the tray, into your hand and move your hand to Simon's. Move Simon to Peter and John and continue:

and said, "Sell me this power so I can give the Holy Spirit."

Open your hand and offer the money to Peter and John.

Peter became angry and scolded him. "Simon, you cannot buy the Holy Spirit. The Holy Spirit is a gift. It is not magic power."

Close your hand to hide the money and place the money back in the basket.

"The Holy Spirit is a gift from God."

Responding to God's Word: Wondering Together

I wonder how Simon feels hearing that he cannot buy the power to give the Holy Spirit?

I wonder how the people feel about Simon?

I wonder how these people are feeling as they receive the gift of the Holy Spirit?

I wonder what they will do with this gift?

I wonder how the people feel following Jesus instead of Simon?

I wonder how the people feel who were healed?

I wonder what they will do now that they are healed?

Return to the Worship Center Order and continue. The scripture reading is Acts 8:4–25. (Select verses to read.)

MATERIALS

1. Wooden tray
2. Three baskets for figures and coins: one for Simon the magician and coins; one for Philip, Peter, and John; one for other figures
3. Cashmere tan felt underlay: 36" by 24"
4. Denim felt stream (Cut one piece of denim felt, 6" wide and 30" long, for the stream; see diagram—stream curves a little. Cut a second piece of denim felt, 6" wide and 15" long, to be glued atop half of the longer piece. Place the second piece at the end of the first, longer piece and glue or sew together only the sides and the end of the felt. Leave the part in the middle of the stream open so figures can be slipped between the two pieces of felt to represent baptism.)
5. Wooden city wall:* 14" by 7", with two sides 4" by 7" glued to the back of the wall to support it
6. Wooden figures:*   ***Standing***—Philip, man, woman with unclean spirit, paralyzed woman, lame boy (made so that crutch can be removed), Simon the magician, Peter, and John
7. A handful of interesting coins (preferably from Israel; purchase from a coin shop)

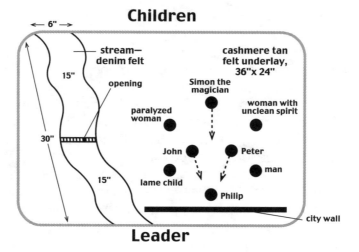

Children

6"

stream—
denim felt

cashmere tan
felt underlay,
36"x 24"

15"

opening

Simon the
magician

woman with
unclean spirit

paralyzed
woman

30"

John

Peter

15"

man

lame child

Philip

city wall

Leader

32

Dorcas, Follower of Jesus, Helps the Poor in Judea

Acts 9:36–42

*Walk slowly to the shelf and pick up the tray with the materials for **Dorcas, Follower of Jesus, Helps the Poor in Judea.** Carry it carefully to the circle and set the tray beside you. Take the french vanilla felt underlay and lay it out in front of you. Smooth it and trace it as you say:*

This is part of the land of Judea. So many important things happen in Judea that we need a small piece of it to help us tell the stories.

Place the house at the center of the underlay near the edge closest to you. Place the mat on the center edge of the floor on the ground level of the house. Place the bed against the wall of the upper level of the house, so there is room for Dorcas and Peter to stand there. Then pause for a moment and say:

When the gift of the Holy Spirit was given to Jesus' followers, they were filled with so much love that amazing things happened. They did what Jesus would do. They did this in Jerusalem, in Samaria, and now in Judea.

Present Dorcas, and hold her while you say:

When Dorcas received the gift of the Holy Spirit, she did what Jesus would do but in her own special way.

Place Dorcas in front of her mat.

Dorcas helped the widows . . .

Present a widow, and place her at the end of the mat to your right and continue:

and the poor.

Present a poor woman, and place her at the end of the mat to your left.

She made clothes for them.

Present a tunic and lay it on the underlay in front of the house to your right.

175

Present another tunic and lay it to your left of the first one. Continue until five tunics are displayed.

But one day, Dorcas became very sick.

Lay her on the mat.

She was dying.

Pause, feeling sad, look at her.

When she died, the women washed her.

Wash her.

And they laid her in a room upstairs.

Lay her on your left hand and place your right hand over the lower part of her body to hold her as you carry Dorcas up the steps. Place her on the bed. Cover her with a white linen cloth.

Meanwhile other disciples sent for Peter.

Take Peter from the tray and move him from the right-center edge of the underlay to Dorcas' house.

When Peter arrived, the women were crying. They showed Peter the clothes Dorcas had made for them.

Glide your hand above the clothes. Then move Peter up the steps to Dorcas.

Peter began praying.

Pause a while, to represent Peter's time of praying, then say:

Turning toward her, . . .

Turn Peter toward Dorcas.

Peter said, "Dorcas, get up."

Pause.

Dorcas opened her eyes. Peter took her hand, helped her up, and she could stand.

Gently stand her up, and move them to face the "people."

Peter called to the people, "Look. Dorcas is alive."

Pause.

Then many believed that Jesus was the Christ. And they began to follow Jesus and the way of the kingdom of God.

Responding to God's Word: Wondering Together

I wonder how the people are feeling when Dorcas is dying?

I wonder how the people feel seeing Dorcas alive again?

I wonder what it was like for Dorcas to die and to be made alive again?

I wonder how Dorcas feels?

I wonder what Peter said when he prayed to God?

I wonder how the people might feel about Jesus if Dorcas had not been made alive again?

I wonder what it means for these people to believe that Jesus is the Christ?

I wonder what they will do in their own special ways to show their love for God and others?

Return to the Worship Center Order and continue. The scripture reading is Acts 9:36–42.

MATERIALS

1. Wooden tray
2. Four baskets: one for Dorcas and the tunics; one for the widow and poor woman; one for Peter; one for the water jar and cotton balls
3. French vanilla felt underlay: 36″ by 24″
4. Wooden figures:*   **Standing**—Dorcas, widow, poor woman, and Peter
5. Tunics* (make five)
6. White linen cloth for covering Dorcas: 5″ by 6″
7. Dorcas's house*

8. Mat: 4½″ by 2½″, made of woven fabric or tweed
9. Bed:* solid piece of wood, 4½″ by 2½″ by 1¾″
10. White felt sheet to cover the bed: 4½″ by 2½″
11. Small water jar (purchase from a craft shop)
12. Cotton balls for washing Dorcas

Children

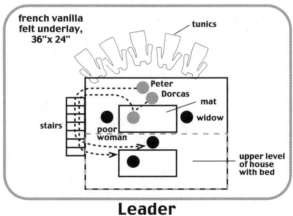

Leader

33

John, Follower of Jesus,
Teaches throughout the World

Revelation 21:1–4

Walk slowly to the shelf and pick up the tray with the materials for **John, Follower of Jesus, Teaches Throughout the World.** *Carry it carefully to the circle and set the tray beside you. Take the crystal blue and pirate green underlay and lay it out in front of you. Smooth it. Place the pirate green felt island of Patmos on the blue part (offshore of Ephesus) on the underlay to your right. (Please see diagram.) Then trace with your finger the edges of the green part of the underlay that represents the mainland, as you say:*

This is a part of the nations of the world. So many important things happen here that we need a small piece of it to help us tell the stories.

Sit back and pause. Then say:

After Jesus went away so he could be with us always, in every time and every place, Jesus' followers received God's gift of the Holy Spirit. They were filled with so much love that they went throughout the world telling the good news of Jesus the Christ and showing the way of the kingdom of God.
Some went to Jerusalem.

Present and lay flat on the area of the underlay representing Palestine the marker with the word "Jerusalem" written on it. (Please see diagram.)

Some went to Judea.

Present and lay on the land the marker with the word "Judea" written on it.

Some went to Samaria.

Present and lay on the land the marker with the word "Samaria" written on it.

And some went to all the nations.

Trace with your finger a path across the green area representing Asia Minor.

John . . .

Present John and place him by the Jerusalem marker.

went far away to the city of Ephesus.

Present and lay on the area representing Ephesus the marker with the word "Ephesus" written on it.

As John traveled to Ephesus,

Begin moving John slowly from Jerusalem toward Samaria. When he is past Samaria stop him and say:

he helped many people believe that Jesus was the Christ, . . .

Move John slowly into Asia Minor, stop, and say:

and he showed them the way of the kingdom of God.

Slowly continue moving John. Stop and say:

The people began to love God and each other so much that they met together in groups, called churches, to worship God.

Trace a circle in front of John with your finger to represent a church. Then move John on to Ephesus and say:

But while John was teaching about Jesus and the kingdom of God in Ephesus, some people didn't like what he was saying. They arrested him.

Bind John with tape.

They took John by boat to the island of Patmos.

Cup your left hand like a boat and with your right hand place and hold John in the "boat." Glide your left hand on the "water" to the island of Patmos. Place John on the island and say:

He couldn't go home.

Place a small linked chain encircling the island.

John was in exile.

Remove the binding from John and sit him down.

It wasn't safe for John to write to his friends. So he used a secret code that only the churches of the followers of Jesus could understand. John wrote to them his special vision of the kingdom of God.

Place a bright yellow felt circle on the center of the blue underlay. Take the scroll from the tray, unroll it, present it, and say:

This is part of John's vision of the kingdom of God that he wrote to the churches in a secret code. Listen to what John wrote:

Turn the writing toward you and read slowly from the scroll, giving everyone time to imagine this vision.

"I saw a new heaven and a new earth. And I saw the new Jerusalem, coming down out of heaven from God, and I heard a loud voice from the throne saying, 'Behold, the dwelling of God is with people. God will live with them, and they shall be God's people. God will wipe away every tear from their eyes, there shall be no death, there shall be no sadness, or crying, or pain anymore. The old way is gone. . . . God is making everything new.' "

Place the scroll on the yellow felt circle.

Responding to God's Word: Wondering Together

I wonder how the people John wrote to feel about the secret message?

I wonder what they like most about John's vision of the kingdom of God?

I wonder what the churches' visions of the kingdom of God are like?

I wonder what they would write to John that would tell him their vision of the kingdom of God?

I wonder what words they would use to disguise their vision of the kingdom of God?

I wonder what they might draw to show their vision of the kingdom of God?

Return to the Worship Center Order and continue. The scripture reading is Revelation 21:1–4.

MATERIALS

1. Wooden tray
2. Three baskets: one for John; one for the chain; one for the signs
3. Wooden figure of John* (Cut the hole for the dowel before cutting the figure; see pattern.)
4. Crystal blue felt underlay: 37" by 27"

5. Pirate green felt mainland* (Glue or sew it to the blue felt underlay.)
6. Pirate green felt island of Patmos*
7. Signs* for Jerusalem, Judea, Samaria, and Ephesus
8. Chain: with 1½" links and 32" long, to encircle Patmos
9. Bright yellow felt circle: 20" in diameter
10. Scroll* with Revelation 21:1–4 printed on it
11. Tape for binding John (⅓" correction and cover-up tape)

Children

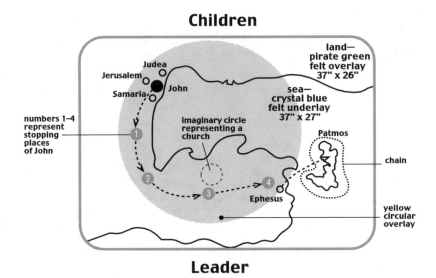

Leader

34

A New Heaven, a New Earth, and a New Jerusalem

Revelation 21:22–26

Walk slowly to the shelf and pick up the tray with the materials for **A New Heaven, a New Earth, and a New Jerusalem.** *Carry it carefully to the circle and set the tray beside you. Take the crystal blue and pirate green underlay and lay it out in front of you. Smooth it. Place the pirate green felt island of Patmos on the blue part (offshore of Ephesus) on the underlay to your right. (Please see diagram.) Then trace with your finger the edge of the green part of the underlay that represents the mainland, as you say:*

This is a part of the nations of the world. So many important things happen here that we need a small piece of it to help us tell the stories.

Sit back and pause. Then say:

After Jesus went away so he could be with us always, in every time and every place, Jesus' followers received God's gift of the Holy Spirit. They were filled with so much love that they went throughout the world telling the good news of Jesus the Christ and showing the way of the kingdom of God.
Some went to Jerusalem.

Present and lay flat on the area of the underlay representing Palestine the marker with the word "Jerusalem" written on it. (Please see diagram.)

Some went to Judea.

Present and lay on the land the marker with the word "Judea" written on it.

Some went to Samaria.

Present and lay on the land the marker with the word "Samaria" written on it.

And some went to all the nations.

Trace with your finger a path across the green area representing Asia Minor.

John . . .

Present John and place him by the Jerusalem marker.

went far away to the city of Ephesus.

Present and lay on the area representing Ephesus the marker with the word "Ephesus" written on it.

As John traveled to Ephesus,

Begin moving John slowly from Jerusalem toward Samaria. When he is past Samaria stop him and say:

he helped many people believe that Jesus was the Christ, . . .

Move John slowly into Asia Minor, stop, and say:

and he showed them the way of the kingdom of God.

Slowly continue moving John. Stop and say:

The people began to love God and each other so much that they met together in groups, called churches, to worship God.

Trace a circle in front of John with your finger to represent a church. Then move John on to Ephesus and say:

But while John was teaching about Jesus and the kingdom of God in Ephesus, some people didn't like what he was saying. They arrested him.

Bind John with tape.

They took John by boat to the island of Patmos.

Cup your left hand like a boat and with your right hand place and hold John in the "boat." Glide your left hand on the "water" to the island of Patmos. Place John on the island and say:

He couldn't go home.

Place a small linked chain encircling the island.

John was in exile.

Remove the binding from John and sit him down.

It wasn't safe for John to write to his friends. So he used a secret code that only the churches of the followers of Jesus could understand. John wrote to them his special vision of the kingdom of God.

Place a bright yellow felt circle on the center of the underlay. Take the scroll from the tray, unroll it, present it, and say:

This is part of John's vision of the kingdom of God that he wrote to the churches in a secret code. He wrote:

Turn the writing toward you and read slowly from the scroll, giving everyone time to imagine this vision.

"I saw a new heaven and a new earth. And I saw the holy city, the new Jerusalem. . . . And I saw no temple in the city, for its temple is God. And the city has no need of sun or moon to shine upon it, for the glory of God is its light. By its light shall the nations walk; and the rulers of the earth will bring their glory into it, and its gates shall never be shut by day—and there shall be no night there; they need no light of lamp or sun, for God will be their light, and they shall reign for ever and ever."

Place the scroll on the yellow circle.

Responding to God's Word:
Wondering Together

I wonder what the churches John wrote to think this secret message means?

I wonder how the people John wrote to feel about the secret message?

I wonder what they think John means when he writes, "God will be their light"?

I wonder how they feel about God being their light in the new Jerusalem?

I wonder how they feel about living in such a place?

I wonder what they would write to John that would tell him how they feel about his message?

I wonder what they might draw to show John how they feel about his message?

Return to the Worship Center Order and continue. The scripture reading is Revelation 21:22–26.

MATERIALS

1. Wooden tray
2. Three baskets: one for John; one for the chain; one for the signs
3. Wooden figure of John* (Cut the hole for the dowel before cutting the figure; see pattern for session 33.)
4. Crystal blue felt underlay: 37" by 27"
5. Pirate green felt mainland* (Glue or sew it to the blue felt underlay; use pattern for session 33.)
6. Pirate green felt island of Patmos* (use pattern for session 33.)
7. Signs* for Jerusalem, Judea, Samaria, and Ephesus (see patterns for session 33.)
8. Chain: 1½" links and 32" long to encircle Patmos
9. Bright yellow felt circle: 20" in diameter
10. Scroll* with Revelation 21:22–26 printed on it
11. Tape for binding John (⅓" correction and cover-up tape)

Children

Leader

APPENDIXES

Appendix A
Telling Stories over Fifty-two Weeks

God's Gift of Jesus the Christ
1. Baby Jesus Is Presented to God
2. Repeat Baby Jesus Is Presented to God

Jesus Shows the Way
of the Kingdom of God in Galilee
3. Follow Me
4. A New Teaching
5. Jesus and the Paralytic
6. Repeat Jesus and the Paralytic
7. Jesus and the Tax Collectors
8. Jesus Calls the Twelve Disciples
9. Repeat Jesus Calls the Twelve Disciples
10. The Parable of the Farmer and the Growing Seed
11. Repeat The Parable of the Farmer and the Growing Seed
12. The Parable of the Treasure
13. Repeat The Parable of the Treasure
14. The Parable of the Fishnet
15. Repeat The Parable of the Fishnet
16. Jesus and the Storm
17. Repeat Jesus and the Storm
18. Jesus Heals Two "Daughters"
19. Repeat Jesus Heals Two "Daughters"
20. Jesus Feeds Five Thousand People
21. Repeat Jesus Feeds Five Thousand People
22. The Transfiguration of Jesus
23. Repeat The Transfiguration of Jesus
24. Jesus Heals a Boy
25. Who Is the Greatest?

Jesus Shows the Way
of the Kingdom of God in Jerusalem
26. Jesus Makes Lazarus Alive Again
27. Repeat Jesus Makes Lazarus Alive Again
28. The Parable of the Two Sons

29. Repeat The Parable of the Two Sons
30. The Most Important Commandment
31. Repeat The Most Important Commandment
32. The Gift of the Poor Widow
33. A Woman Anoints Jesus for Burial
34. Repeat A Woman Anoints Jesus for Burial
35. Too Afraid to Follow Jesus
36. Jesus' Trial
37. Jesus Dies and God Makes Jesus Alive Again
38. Jesus Appears to Mary Magdalene
39. Jesus Appears to Thomas

*Jesus' Disciples Show the Way of the Kingdom of God
in Jerusalem, Judea, Samaria, and the World*

40. Jesus Commissions the Disciples
41. Repeat Jesus Commissions the Disciples
42. Jesus Appears to the Disciples by the Sea
43. Jesus Again Asks Peter to Follow Him
44. God's Gift of the Holy Spirit
45. Repeat God's Gift of the Holy Spirit
46. Peter, Follower of Jesus, Heals a Lame Man in Jerusalem
47. Philip, Follower of Jesus, Teaches in Samaria
48. Repeat Philip, Follower of Jesus, Teaches in Samaria
49. Dorcas, Follower of Jesus, Helps the Poor in Judea
50. Repeat Dorcas, Follower of Jesus, Helps the Poor in Judea
51. John, Follower of Jesus, Teaches throughout the World
52. A New Heaven, a New Earth, and a New Jerusalem

Appendix B

COVERING A PARABLE BOX WITH GOLD PAPER

1. To cover the inside bottom of a parable box:

   - Cut a piece of gold foil wrapping paper, which measures the length of the box plus two inches, and the width plus two inches.
   - Tape the paper to the inside bottom of the box so the paper extends up each side one inch.

2. Repeat the above procedure to cover the inside of the lid.

3. To cover the rest of the box:

   - Cut a piece of gold foil wrapping paper, which measures the length of the box plus four times the height of the box and the width of the box plus four times the height of the box. This will cover the inside as well as the outside of the box.
   - Place the box on the wrapping paper. Place the edge of the paper at the edge of the height of the box and make a crease on the paper along the bottom length of the box.
   - Do the same on the opposite side of the length of the box.
   - Then place the edge of the paper at the edge of the height of the box and make a crease on the paper along the bottom width of the box.
   - Remove the box from the paper and fold the paper at the creases along the length and the width.
   - Place the box in the middle of the paper and place the creased part at the top edge of the height of the box. Fold the paper into the box so that the entire box is covered.

4. Repeat the above procedure to cover the lid.

Appendix C

MATERIALS FOR FOLLOWING JESUS

TOTAL QUANTITY	ITEM	SESSION # (quantity)	PATTERN PAGE #

MATERIALS FOR THE CENTRAL SHELF

Incarnation

    1   Nativity set
(See *Young Children and Worship* pages 143–146 for the above story.)

Satin cloths to set under the nativity set:
    2   Advent: Blue or purple
    2   Christmas: White
    2   Ordinary time: Green
            (after Epiphany and Pentecost)
    2   Lent: Purple
    2   Easter: White
    2   Pentecost: Red

Baptism

    1   White Christ candle (3″ × 9″ or larger)
    1   Brass candle holder for the Christ candle
1/person   White candle (¾″–1″ × 6″
1/person   Candle holders
    1   White satin cloth to set under the Christ candle
    1   Baptismal bowl
            Wooden figures representing ages your church baptizes
    1   Candle snuffer
    1   White satin underlay (36″ × 24″)
    1   Covered glass container for matches
    1   Tray for candles, matches, and candle snuffer
    1   Tray for baptismal bowl and people figures
(See *Young Children and Worship* pages 72–74 and 212–214 for the above stories.)

Eucharist
1	Good Shepherd
10	Sheep
1	Sheepfold
1	Good Shepherd's table
5	Adults
5	Children
1	Small chalice
1	Plate with clay bread

(See *Young Children and Worship* pages 201–208 for the above story.)

WOODEN TRAYS AND BASKETS

| 28 | Wooden trays | 1, 2, 3, 4, 5, 6, 10, 11, 12, 13, 14, 15,16, 18, 19, 20, 21, 22, 23, 24, 25, 26,27/28, 29, 30, 31, 32, 33/34 |

| 87 | Baskets | 1(2), 2(5), 3(5), 4(5), 5(5), 6(2), 10(1),11(3), 12(3), 13(2), 14(3), 15(2) 16(2), 18(2), 19(5), 20(3), 21(6), 22(4), 23(3), 24(2), 25(2), 26(2), 27/28(4), 29(3), 30(1), 31(3), 32(4), 33/34(3) |

(The size of the baskets will vary depending on the number and size of the material placed in them. See the Materials section of the session for a breakdown of what goes in each basket.)

| 1 | Flat basket (3″) | 12 |
| 12 | Tiny woven oval-shaped baskets (1½″ × 1″ × ¾″) | 12 |

STANDING WOODEN FIGURES

Total Quantity	Item	Session # (quantity)	Pattern Page #
1	Mary, Jesus' mother	1	206
1	Baby Jesus	1	206
1	Joseph	1	206
1	Simeon	1	206
1	Anna	1	206
13	Jesus	2, 3, 5, 6, 10, 11, 12, 13, 14, 16, 21, 22, 23	208
3	Poor woman	2, 3, 32	208
2	Sick man	2, 3	208
4	Girl	2, 3, 5, 25	208

TOTAL QUANTITY	ITEM	SESSION # (quantity)	PATTERN PAGE #
4	Boy	2, 3, 5, 25	208
17	Peter	2, 3, 5, 6, 10, 11, 12, 13, 14, 21, 25, 26, 27/28, 30, 31,32	209
13	Andrew	2, 3, 5, 6, 10, 12, 13, 14, 21, 25, 26, 27/28	210
14	James	2, 3, 5, 6, 10, 11, 12, 13, 14, 21, 25, 26, 27/28	210
16	John	2, 3, 5, 6, 10, 11, 12, 13, 14, 21, 25, 26, 27/28, 30, 31	209
7	Scribes	3(2), 5(2), 21, 22, 23	211
1	Man with unclean spirit	3	211
1	Paralytic	4	213
1	woman	5	219
7	Levi, (Matthew)	5, 6, 12, 13, 14, 21, 26	219
10	Philip	6, 10, 12, 13, 14, 21, 26, 27/28, 31	221
8	Bartholomew (Nathanael)	6, 12, 13, 14, 21, 26, 27/28	221
10	Thomas	6, 10, 12, 13, 14, 21, 25, 26, 27/28	221
6	James	6, 12, 13, 14, 21, 26	221
6	Thaddaeus	6, 12, 13, 14, 21, 26	222
6	Simon	6, 12, 13, 14, 21, 26	222
6	Judas	6, 12, 13, 14, 21, 22	222
1	Jesus bending	10	238
1	Jairus	11	239
1	Mother	11	239
1	Daughter	11	240
1	Bleeding woman	11	239
1	Father	14	242
1	Son	14	242
1	Lazarus	16	245
1	Mary	16	245
1	Martha	16	245
1	Teacher of the law	18	248
5	Elders	19, 21, 22(2), 23	252
2	Rich women	19	251
1	Rich man	19	252
1	Rich girl	19	251
1	Rich boy	19	251
1	Poor widow	19	252
5	Chief priests	19, 21, 22(2), 23	252

TOTAL QUANTITY	ITEM	SESSION # (quantity)	PATTERN PAGE #
1	Woman who anoints Jesus	20	253
3	Soldiers	21, 22, 23	254
2	Caiaphas	21, 22	255
1	Servant girl	21	254
2	Bystanders	21	254
1	Pilate	23	257
1	Joseph of Arimathea	23	257
3	Mary Magdalene	23, 24, 25	257
3	Mary, mother of James and Joses	23, 24, 25	257
3	Salome	23, 24, 25	257
2	Mary, mother of Jesus	23, 25	259
2	Jesus with outstretched hands	23, 26	259
1	Young man	24	260
3	Jesus with nail marks	24, 25, 27/28	260
1	Joanna	25	261
1	Lame man	30	267
1	Man	31	268
1	Woman with unclean spirit	31	268
1	Paralyzed woman	31	268
1	Lame boy	31	268
1	Simon the magician	31	268
1	Dorcas	32	270
1	Widow	32	270
1	John bending	33/34	272

SITTING WOODEN FIGURES

1	Fisher father, Zebedee	2, 4	209
2	Fisher servant	2, 4	209
3	Andrew	4, 15, 20	216
6	Jesus	4, 5, 15, 18, 19, 20	213
5	Peter	4, 15, 18, 19, 20	215

TOTAL QUANTITY	ITEM	SESSION # (quantity)	PATTERN PAGE #
5	James	4, 15, 18, 19, 20	216
5	John	4, 15, 18, 19, 20	216
6	Women	4(3), 5 (3)	215
1	Girl	4	213
1	Boy	4	213
1	Poor woman	4	214
1	Sick man	4	213
1	Lonely person	4	214
1	Rich woman	4	214
1	Farmer	4	214
2	Scribe	4	213
3	Levi (Matthew)	5, 15, 20	218
2	Men sinners, tax collectors	5	218
3	Sitting crowd	6	223–24
2	Philip	15, 20	243
2	Bartholomew (Nathanael)	15, 20	243
2	Thomas	15, 20	243
2	James	15, 20	243
2	Thaddaeus	15, 20	244
2	Simon	15, 20	244
2	Judas	15, 20	244
1	Child	15	244
1	Chief priest	18	248
1	Elder	18	248
1	Simon the leper	20	253

BUILDINGS AND BACKGROUNDS

TOTAL QUANTITY	ITEM	SESSION # (quantity)	PATTERN PAGE #
5	Temples	1, 18, 19, 22, 30	207
1	Synagogue	3	212
2	Peter's house with removable roof	4, 15	217
1	Tax Booth	5	219
2	Backdrop (17″ × 6″ × 2″)	5, 20	220
3	Backdrop (11½″ × 6″ × 2″)	11, 16, 23	240
1	Backdrop with doors	25	261
1	Samaria city wall	31	269
1	Dorcas's house	32	271

TOTAL QUANTITY	ITEM	SESSION # (quantity)	PATTERN PAGE #

OTHER WOODEN MATERIALS

4	Boats	2, 6, 10, 27/28	210
2	Round wooden tables (6¾″ × ¾″)	5, 20	

Beds

1	(4¼″ × 2¼″ × 1¼″)	11	
1	(4¼″ × 2¾″ × 1¼″)	16	
1	(4½″ × 2½″ × 1¾″)	32	271
1	Treasury box	19	
3	Olive trees	21	256
1	Platform with cross	23	258
1	Table (8½″ × 3″)	25	261
	Wooden fish	27/28	263

MOUNTAINS AND TOMBS

Mountain in Galilee — 225

2	plaster cloth	6, 26	
	newspaper	6, 26	
	tape	6, 26	
	sponge	6, 26	
	green nontoxic paint	6, 26	
	brown nontoxic paint	6, 26	

Mount of Transfiguration — 241

2	plaster cloth	13, 14	
	newspaper	13, 14	
	tape	13, 14	
	sponge	13, 14	
	gray paint	13, 14	
	brown paint	13, 14	

Lazarus's tomb with stone — 245

1	plaster cloth	16	
	newspaper	16	
	tape	16	
	sponge	16	
1	jeweler's saw or or keyhole saw	16	

| | different shades of gray paint | 16 | |

Jesus tomb with stone — 259

2	plaster cloth newspaper tape sponge	23, 24	
1	jeweler's saw or keyhole saw	23, 24	
	different shades of gray paint	23, 24	

CLAY MATERIALS

2	Platter (4″)	5, 20
8	Goblets	5
5	Clay loaves of bread	12
2	Clay fish	12

LINEN

White linen

2	(4″ × 4″)	16, 23
2	(16″ × 6″)	16, 23
1	(5″ × 6″)	32

CANDLES AND RELATED MATERIALS

7	White taper candles (6″)	29
7	Low brass candle holders	29
1	Covered brass or glass container for burned matches	29
	Safety matches	29
1	Candle snuffer	29

OTHER MATERIALS

1	Fishing nets (15″ × 15″)	2(2), 27/28
2	Tweed mats (4½″ × 2½″)	4, 32

TOTAL QUANTITY	ITEM	SESSION # (quantity)	PATTERN PAGE #
1	Treasure bag: Gold cloth, sequins, and drawstring	8	
1	Black and gold sparkling netting (26″ × 19″)	9	
1	Cushion (4¼″ × 2½″)	10	
2	Water jars	16, 32	
2	Anointing oil	16, 20	
	Cotton balls	16, 32	
26	Various coins	19(20), 31(6)	
2	Tiny copper coins	19	
2	Charcoal fires	21, 27/28	
2	Tape for binding (⅓″ correction and cover-up tape)	21, 33/34	
1	Money bag (4″ × 2″)	22	
30	Silver coins	22	
7	Gift cards	29	265–66
5	Tunics	32	270
1	Set of signs for Jerusalem, Judea, Samaria, and Ephesus	33/34	274
1	Chain with 1½″ links and 32″ long	33/34	

Scrolls

1	Rev. 21:1–4	33	275
1	Rev. 21:22–26	34	276

PARABLE BOXES AND LAMINATED PARABLE MATERIALS

3	Business envelope boxes	7, 8, 9, 17	191
4	Gold wrapping paper	7, 8, 9, 17	191
1	Farmer	7	226
1	Mat	7	227
1	Sickle	7	226
1	Field boundary	8	232–36
1	Person who finds the treasure	8	231

TOTAL QUANTITY	ITEM	SESSION # (quantity)	PATTERN PAGE #
1	Furnishings for the house	8	230–31
1	Sold sign	8	230
8	Fish	9 (two of each)	237
3	Baskets	9, 17(2)	237
1	Vineyard	17	247
1	Father	17	246
2	Sons	17	246

NON-PARABLE LAMINATED MATERIALS

1	White heart-shaped card	18	250
1	Great Commission card	26	262

FELT

The colors and numbers of the felt listed below are from:

Rainbow Classic Felt
Kunin Felt, Foss Manufacturing Company
380 Lafayette Road,
Hampton, NH 03843

Phone: (603) 929-6100
Fax: (603) 929-6180
E-mail: *tjprovencal@flossmfg.com*
Internet home page: *www.kuninfelt.com.* You can view the colors of the felt by clicking on Product Information, then Rainbow Felt Classic. **Note:** Names and colors of fabric are subject to change.

550 White

3	circles (36″)	1, 24, 29
1	circle (11″)	18
1	sheet (4¼″ × 2¼″)	11
1	(4¼ × 2¾″)	16
1	(4½″ × 2½″)	32

Sea of Galilee underlays

9	494 lime green (40″ × 24″)	2, 3, 4, 5, 6, 11, 15, 26, 27/28
9	6J2 blueberry bash (40″ × 24″)	2, 3, 4, 5, 6, 11, 15, 26, 27/28

TOTAL QUANTITY	ITEM	SESSION # (quantity)	PATTERN PAGE #
1	J64 sandstone road	5	
1	353 antique gold underlay (31″ × 36″)	7	
4	Growing grain	7 (one of each stage of growth)	228–29
1	352 gold underlay (33″ × 30″)	8	
1	395 french vanilla village (33″ × 18″)	8	232
1	458 apple green (18″)	9	
1	660 baby blue (18″)	9	
1	6J2 blueberry bash (40″ × 36″)	10	
	494 lime green (34″ × 36″)	12	
2	466 kelly green (36″ × 36″)	13, 14	
2	928 silver gray (36″ × 24″)	16, 20	
1	379 antique white vineyard (28″ × 36″)	17	
1	064 red heart (8″ × 6½″)	18	249
5	J64 sandstone Jerusalem underlay (36″ × 36″)	18, 19, 22, 23, 30	
1	658 navy blue Jerusalem underlay (28″ × 36″)	21	
1	472 hunter green Mount of Olives underlay (12″ × 36″)	21	
2	J65 graystone house outline (12″ × 9″)	21, 22	255

TOTAL QUANTITY	ITEM	SESSION # (quantity)	PATTERN PAGE #
1	458 apple green burial underlay	23	
1	884 cashmere road (30″ × 5″)	24	
1	476 pirate green (36″ × 24″)	25	
3	352 Gold flames (5″ × 20½″)	29	264
	Red 7-tonged flame (22½″ × 34½″)	29	264
4	256 orange flames (5″ × 20½″)	29	264
1	884 cashmere tan (36″ × 24″)	31	
2	J56 denim stream (6″ × 30″, 6″ × 15″)	31	
1	395 french vanilla (36″ × 24″)	32	
1	670 crystal blue (37″ × 27″)	33/34	
1	476 pirate green mainland (36″ × 26″)	33/34	272
1	476 pirate green Patmos (8″ × 5″)	33/34	273
1	351 yellow (20″ diameter)	33/34	

Appendix D

INSTRUCTIONS FOR MAKING PARABLE MATERIALS

1. Find the patterns for the parable materials in the pattern section.
2. Photocopy the patterns.
3. Color them with markers or colored pencils.
4. Arrange them on 8½" × 11" card stock. Leave a border around each figure.
5. Glue them onto the card stock.
6. Take to a color photocopier and have this copied onto card stock making as many copies as you have worship centers. (Save the original for future copying.)
7. Laminate both sides of the patterns.
8. When adhered, cut out the materials along the black lines.

If you cannot color photocopy them, eliminate step 6 and continue.

PATTERNS

Session 1

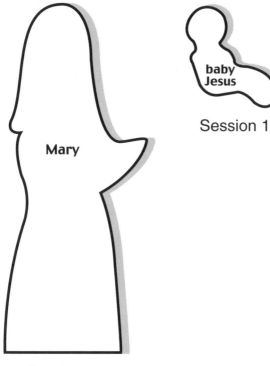

Mary

Session 1

baby Jesus

Session 1

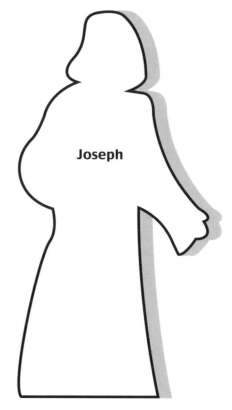

Joseph

Session 1

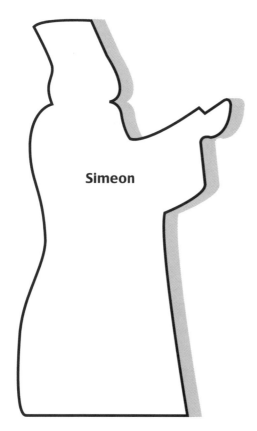

Simeon

Session 1

Anna

Session 1

Session 1

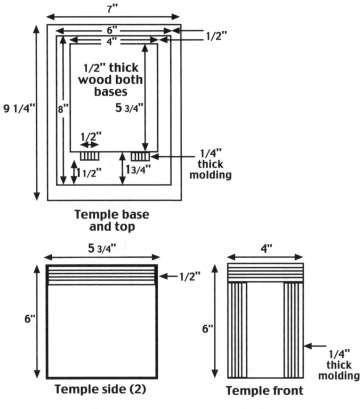

Temple base and top

Temple side (2)

Temple front

Sessions 1, 18, 19, 22, 30

Session 2

boy

Sessions 2, 3, 5, 25

girl

Sessions 2, 3, 5, 25

Jesus

Sessions 2, 3, 5, 6, 10, 11,
12, 13, 14, 16, 21, 22, 23

sick
man

Sessions 2, 3

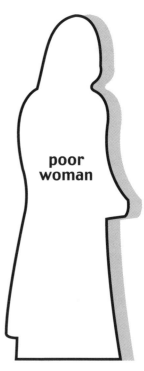

poor
woman

Sessions 2, 3, 32

Session 2

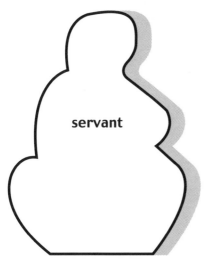

Sessions 2, 4

Sessions 2, 4

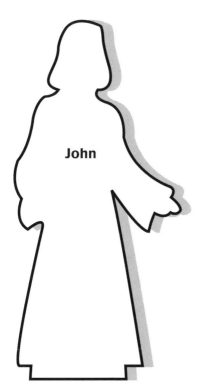

Sessions 2, 3, 5, 6, 10,
11, 12, 13, 14, 21, 25,
26, 27/28, 30, 31

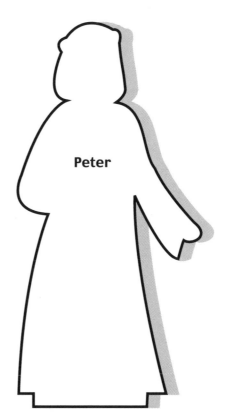

Sessions 2, 3, 5, 6, 10, 11,
12, 13, 14, 21, 25, 26,
27/28, 30, 31, 32

Session 2

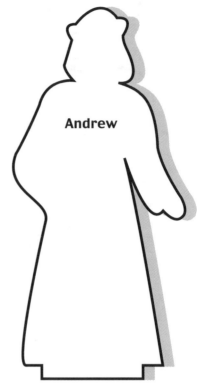

Sessions 2, 3, 5, 6, 10, 11, 12,
13, 14, 21, 25, 26, 27/28

Sessions 2, 3, 5, 6, 10, 12,
13, 14, 21, 25, 26, 27/28

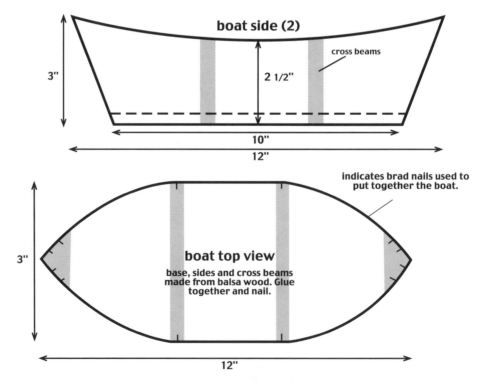

Sessions 2, 6, 10, 27/28

Session 3

Session 3

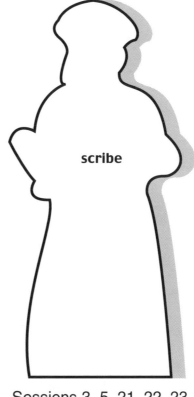

Sessions 3, 5, 21, 22, 23

Session 3

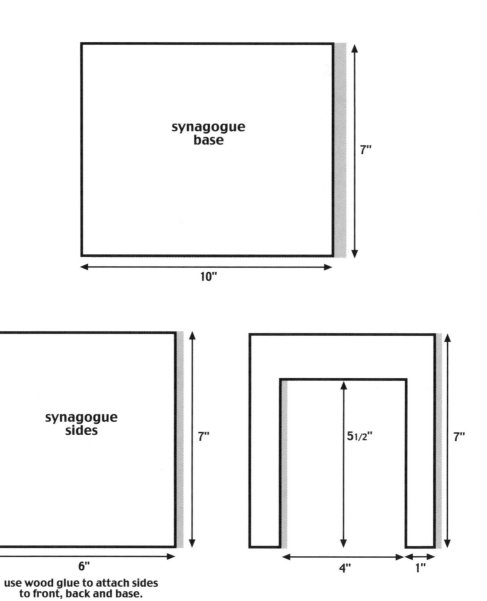

synagogue
base

7"

10"

synagogue
sides

7"

6"

**use wood glue to attach sides
to front, back and base.**

5 1/2"

7"

4"   1"

Session 3

Session 4

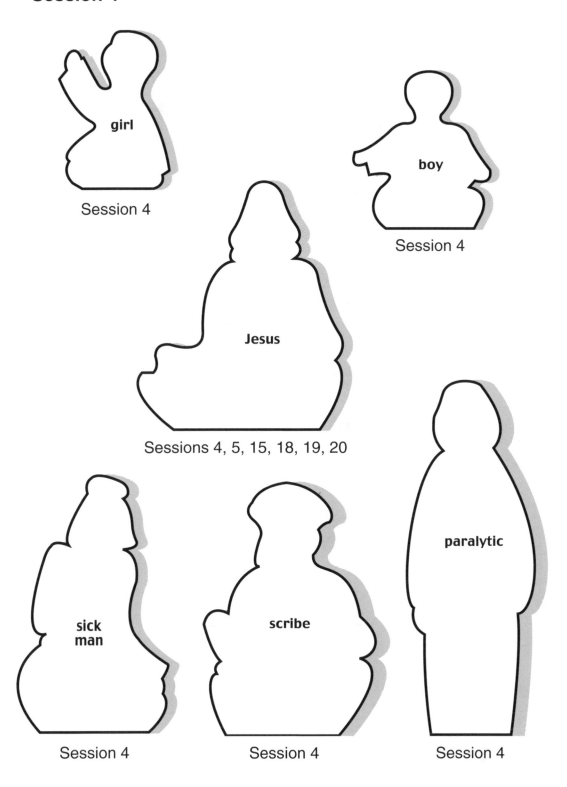

girl

Session 4

boy

Session 4

Jesus

Sessions 4, 5, 15, 18, 19, 20

sick man

Session 4

scribe

Session 4

paralytic

Session 4

Session 4

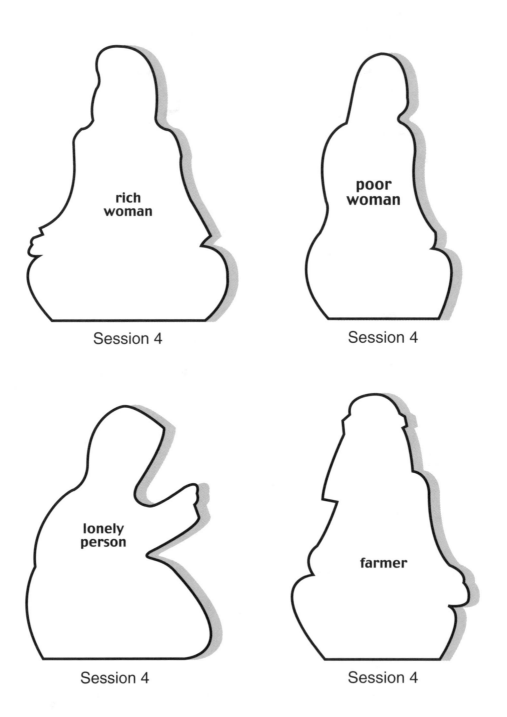

rich
woman

Session 4

poor
woman

Session 4

lonely
person

Session 4

farmer

Session 4

Session 4

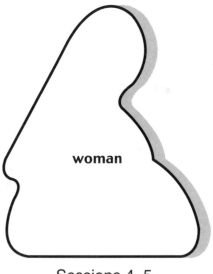

Sessions 4, 5

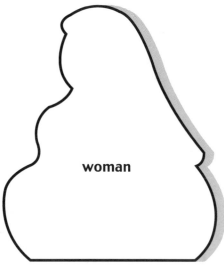

Sessions 4, 5

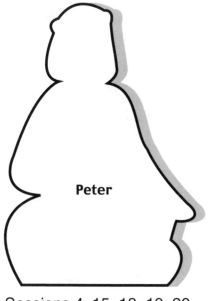

Sessions 4, 15, 18, 19, 20

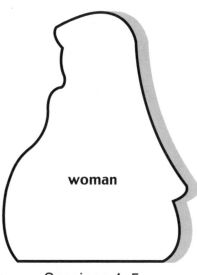

Sessions 4, 5

Session 4

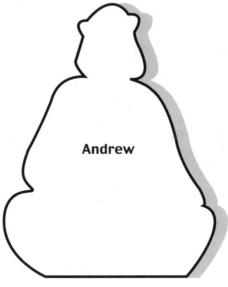

Sessions 4, 15, 20

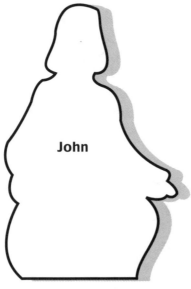

Sessions 4, 15, 18, 19, 20

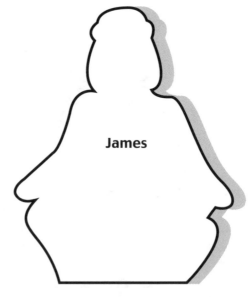

Sessions 4, 15, 18, 19, 20

Session 4

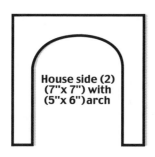

House side (2)
(7"x 7") with
(5"x 6") arch

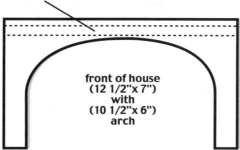

Glue small strips on inside to support
removable roof; line up with back wall.

front of house
(12 1/2"x 7")
with
(10 1/2"x 6")
arch

Peter's roof (12 1/4"x 6 3/4")

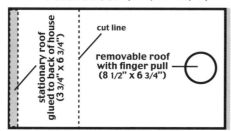

stationary roof
glued to back of house
(3 3/4" x 6 3/4")

cut line

removable roof
with finger pull
(8 1/2" x 6 3/4")

Glue small strips on inside to support
removable roof; line up with front.

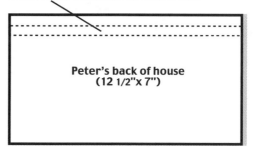

Peter's back of house
(12 1/2"x 7")

Peter's house base
(15"x 9")

Sessions 4, 15

Session 5

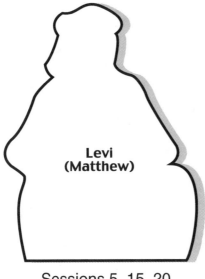

Sessions 5, 15, 20

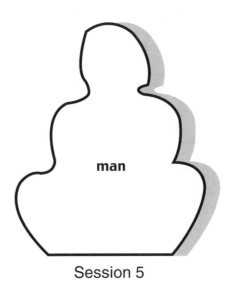

Session 5

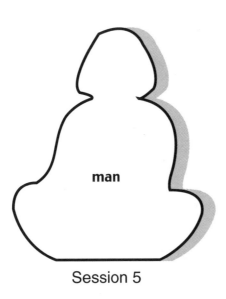

Session 5

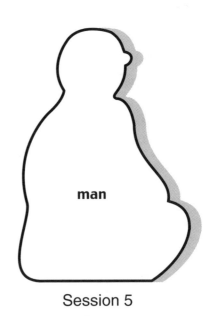

Session 5

Session 5

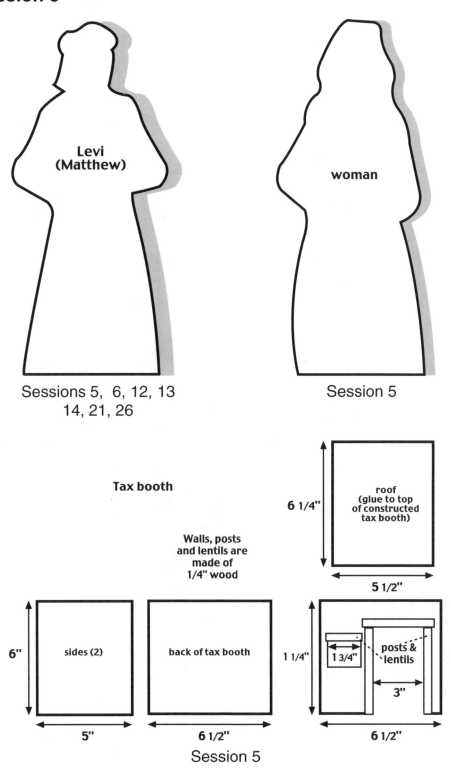

Levi
(Matthew)

Sessions 5, 6, 12, 13
14, 21, 26

woman

Session 5

Tax booth

Walls, posts
and lentils are
made of
1/4" wood

roof
(glue to top
of constructed
tax booth)

6 1/4"

5 1/2"

6"   sides (2)

5"

back of tax booth

6 1/2"

1 1/4"

1 3/4"

posts &
lentils

3"

6 1/2"

Session 5

Session 5

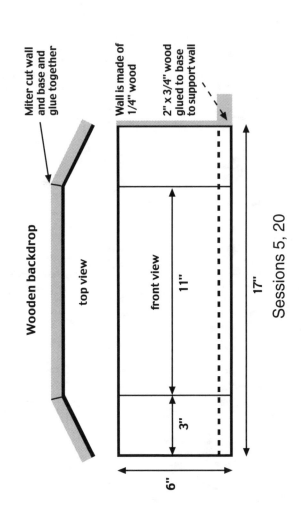

Miter cut wall and base and glue together

Wooden backdrop

top view

Wall is made of 1/4" wood

2" x 3/4" wood glued to base to support wall

front view

11"

3"

17"

6"

Sessions 5, 20

Session 6

Philip

Sessions 6, 10, 12, 13,14,
21, 26, 27/28, 31

Bartholmew
(Nathanael)

Sessions 6, 12, 13, 14,
21, 26, 27/28

Thomas

Sessions 6, 10, 12,
13, 14, 21, 25, 26, 27/28

James

Sessions 6, 12,
13, 14, 21, 26

Session 6

Thaddeus

Simon

Sessions 6, 12, 13, 14, 21, 26   Sessions 6, 12, 13, 14, 21, 26

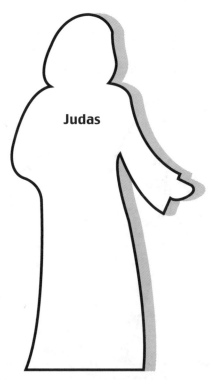

Judas

Sessions 6, 12, 13, 14, 21, 22

Session 6

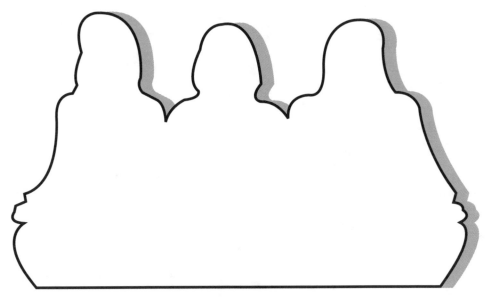

Session 6

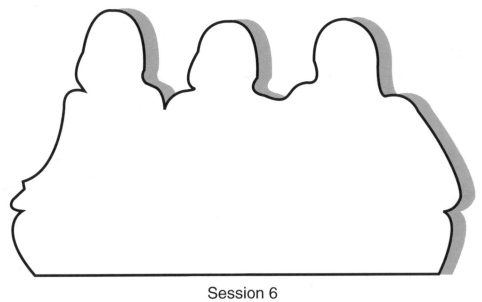

Session 6

Session 6

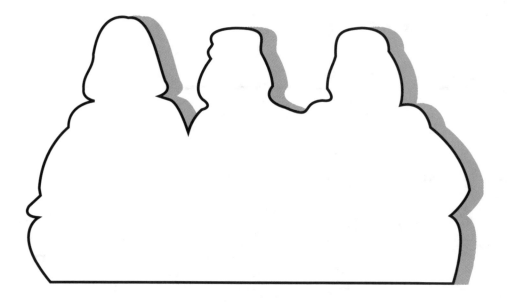

Session 6

Session 6

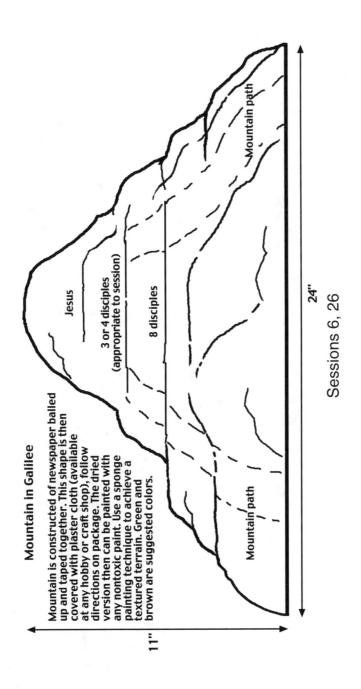

Mountain in Galilee

Mountain is constructed of newspaper balled up and taped together. This shape is then covered with plaster cloth (available at any hobby or craft shop), follow directions on package. The dried version then can be painted with any nontoxic paint. Use a sponge painting technique to achieve a textured terrain. Green and brown are suggested colors.

Jesus

3 or 4 disciples (appropriate to session)

8 disciples

Mountain path

Mountain path

24"

11"

Sessions 6, 26

Session 7

Session 7

Session 7

Session 7

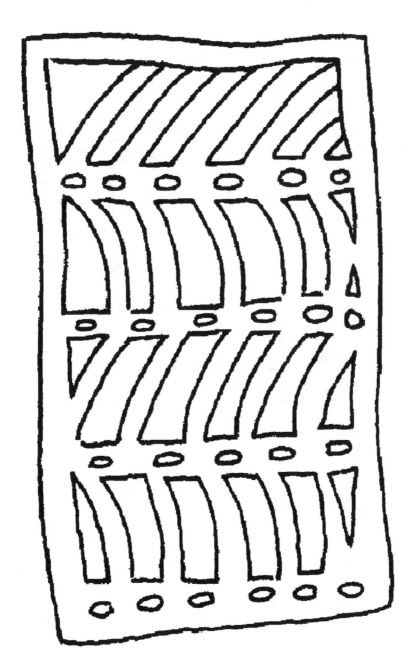

Session 7

Session 7

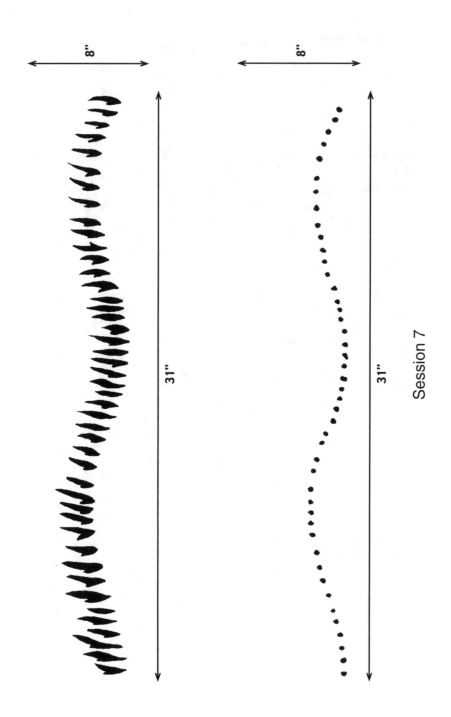

Session 7

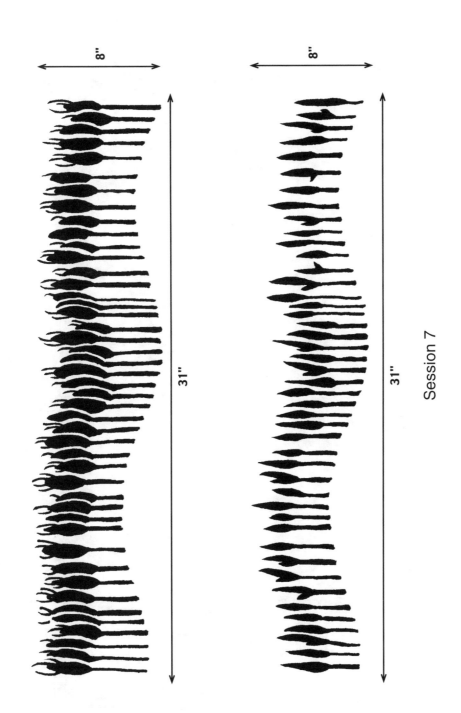

Session 7

Session 8

Session 8

Session 8

Session 8

Session 8

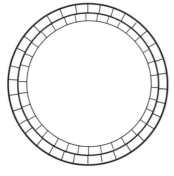

Session 8

Session 8

Session 8

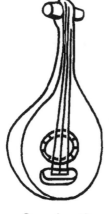

Session 8

Session 8

Session 8

Session 8

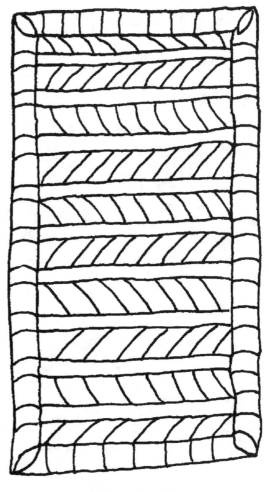

Session 8

Session 8

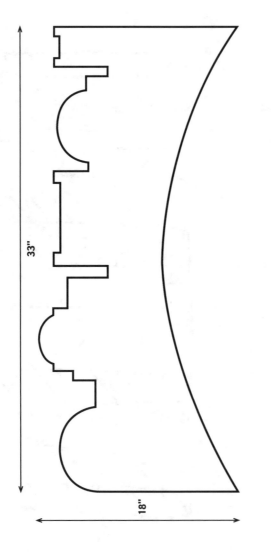

33"

18"

Session 8

Session 8

8 1/4"

Glue or tape edge end-to-end on each section
Glue or tape each field end-to-end

Session 8

4 1/4"

Session 8

8 1/4"

Glue or tape each field end-to-end

Session 8

4 1/4"

Session 8

8 1/4"

Glue or tape each field end-to-end

Session 8

4 1/4"

Session 8

8 1/4"

Glue or tape each field end-to-end

Session 8

4 1/4"

Session 9

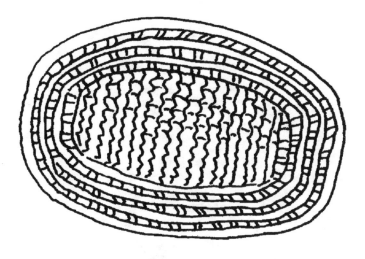

Sessions 9, 17

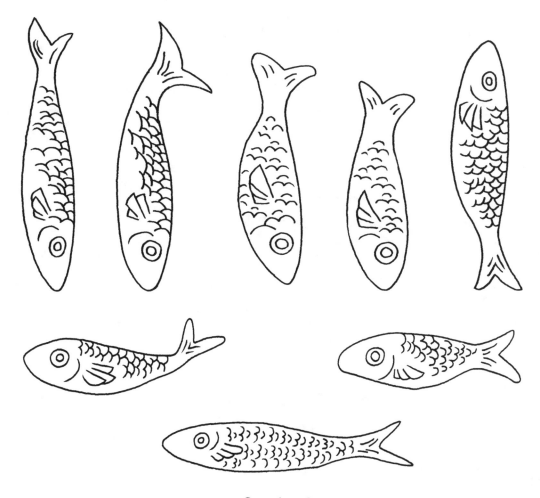

Session 9

Session 10

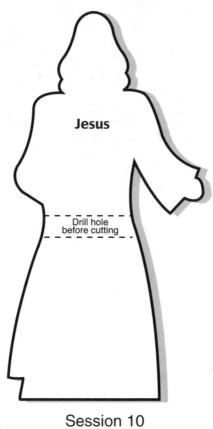

Session 10

Session 11

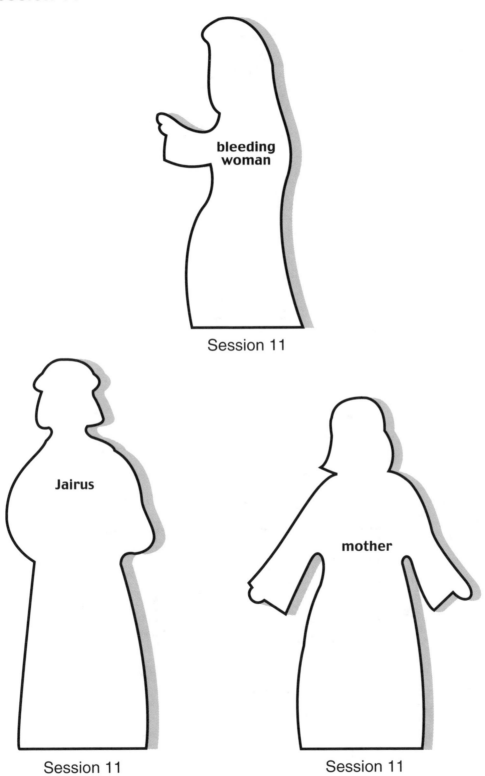

bleeding
woman

Session 11

Jairus

Session 11

mother

Session 11

Session 11

daughter

Session 11

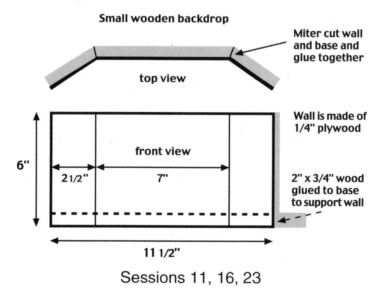

Small wooden backdrop

top view

Miter cut wall
and base and
glue together

front view

Wall is made of
1/4" plywood

6"

2 1/2"

7"

2" x 3/4" wood
glued to base
to support wall

11 1/2"

Sessions 11, 16, 23

Session 13

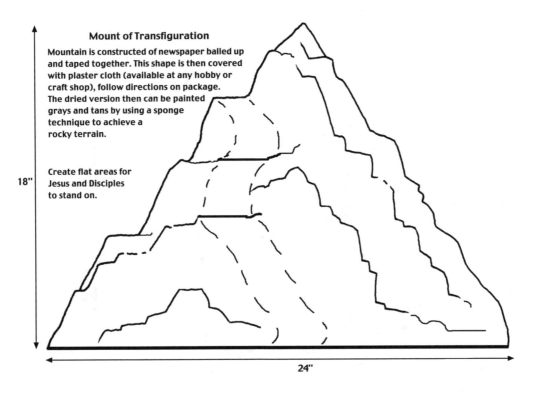

Mount of Transfiguration

Mountain is constructed of newspaper balled up and taped together. This shape is then covered with plaster cloth (available at any hobby or craft shop), follow directions on package. The dried version then can be painted grays and tans by using a sponge technique to achieve a rocky terrain.

Create flat areas for Jesus and Disciples to stand on.

18"

24"

Sessions 13, 14

Session 14

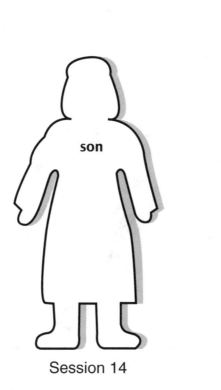

Session 14

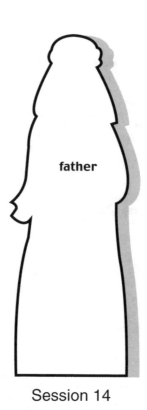

Session 14

Session 15

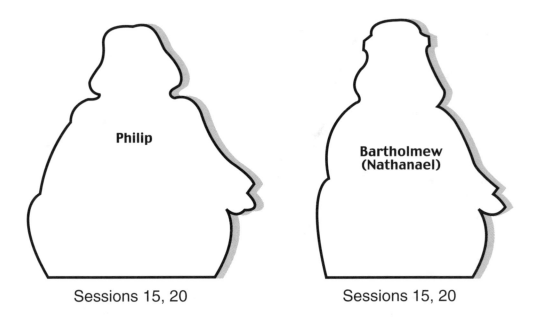

Philip

Sessions 15, 20

Bartholmew
(Nathanael)

Sessions 15, 20

Thomas

Sessions 15, 20

James

Sessions 15, 20

Session 15

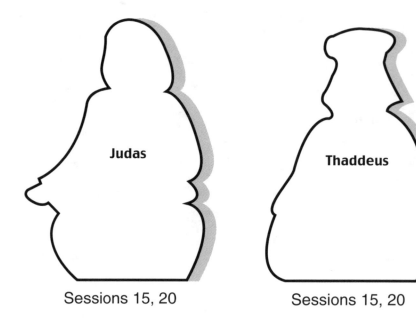

Judas

Sessions 15, 20

Thaddeus

Sessions 15, 20

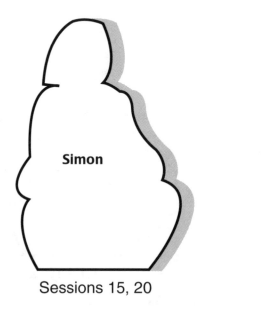

Simon

Sessions 15, 20

child

Session 15

Session 16

Lazarus

Session 16

Mary

Session 16

Martha

Session 16

Lazarus's tomb 16" x 7" x 7"

Tomb is constructed of newspaper balled up and taped together. This shape is then covered with plaster cloth (available at any hobby or craft shop), follow directions on package. After shape dries remove newspaper and tape. Cut opening with jeweler's saw or keyhole saw. The dried version then can be painted grays using a sponge technique to achieve a stone appearance.

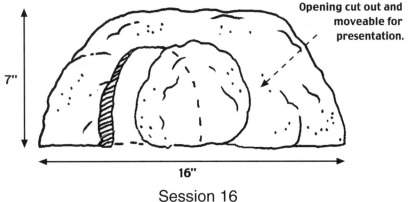

Opening cut out and moveable for presentation.

7"

16"

Session 16

Session 17

Session 17

Session 17   Session 17

20"

26"

Session 17

Session 18

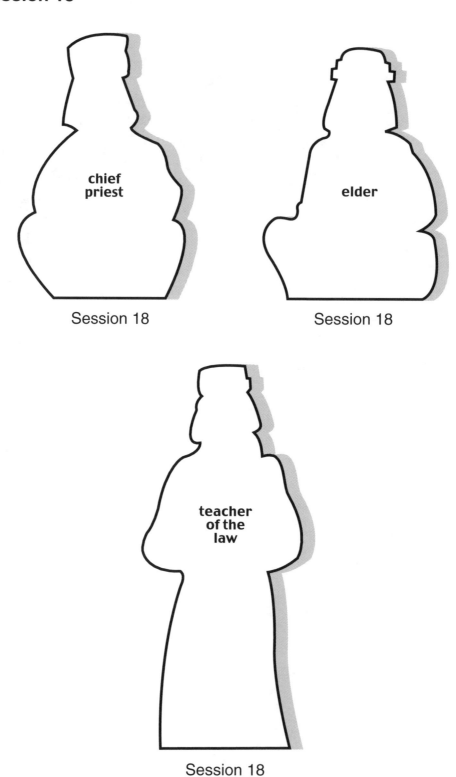

Session 18

Session 18

Session 18

Session 18

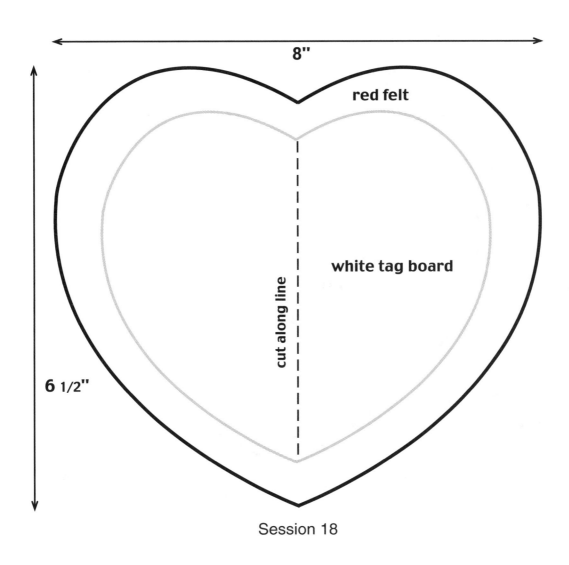

8"

6 1/2"

red felt

white tag board

cut along line

Session 18

Session 18

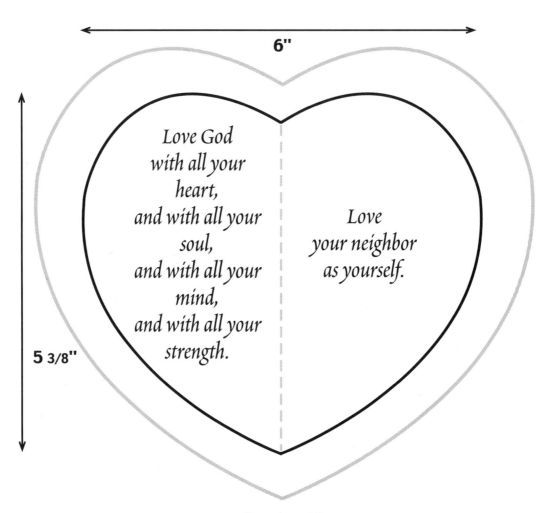

6"

5 3/8"

*Love God
with all your
heart,
and with all your
soul,
and with all your
mind,
and with all your
strength.*

*Love
your neighbor
as yourself.*

Session 18

Session 19

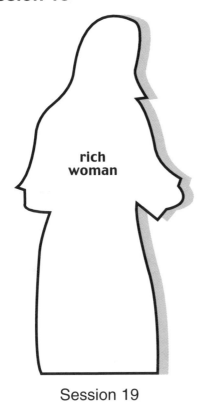

Session 19

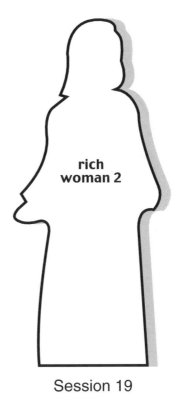

Session 19

Session 19

Session 19

Session 19

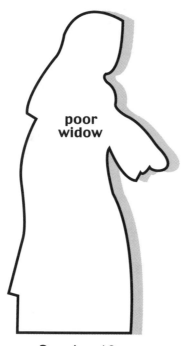

poor
widow

Session 19

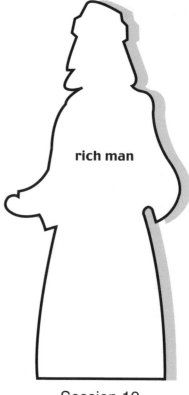

rich man

Session 19

chief
priest

Sessions 19, 21, 22, 23

elder

Sessions 19, 21, 22, 23

Session 20

anointing
woman

Simon
the
leper

Session 20   Session 20

Session 21

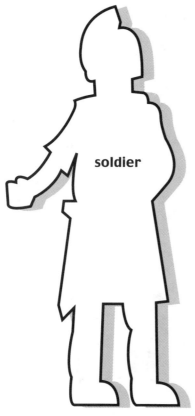

soldier

Sessions 21, 22, 23

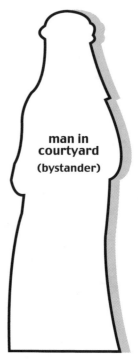

man in
courtyard
(bystander)

Session 21

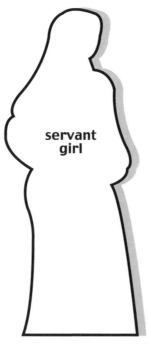

servant
girl

Session 21

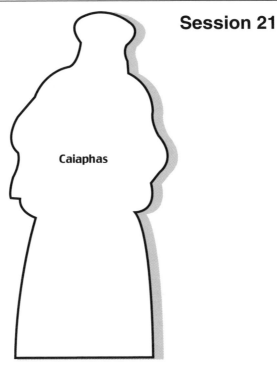

Session 21

Caiaphas

Sessions 21, 22

**Caiaphas's
House**
(12"x 9")
inside of house
(10"x 7")
entry
(2" wide)

Sessions 21, 22

Session 21

olive tree

Session 21

Session 23

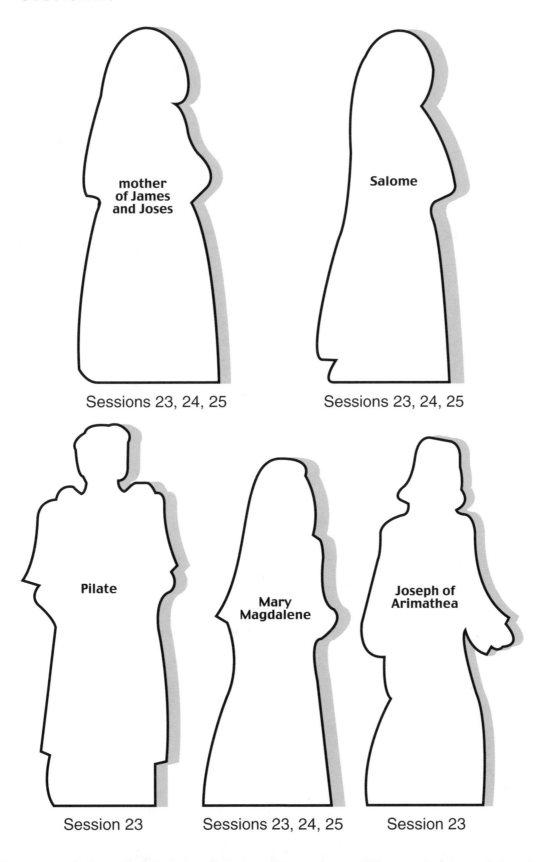

mother
of James
and Joses

Sessions 23, 24, 25

Salome

Sessions 23, 24, 25

Pilate

Session 23

Mary
Magdalene

Sessions 23, 24, 25

Joseph of
Arimathea

Session 23

Session 23

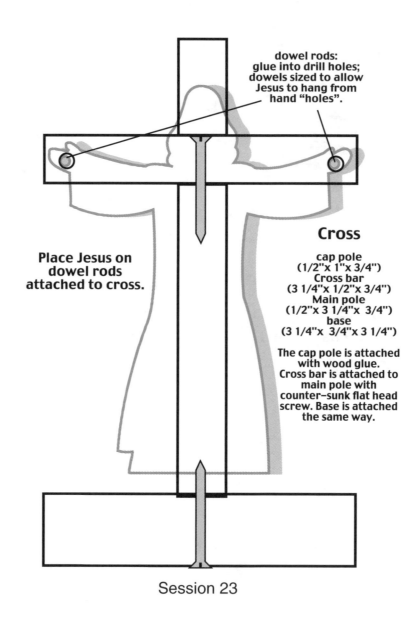

**dowel rods:
glue into drill holes;
dowels sized to allow
Jesus to hang from
hand "holes".**

Cross

**cap pole
(1/2"x 1"x 3/4")
Cross bar
(3 1/4"x 1/2"x 3/4")
Main pole
(1/2"x 3 1/4"x 3/4")
base
(3 1/4"x 3/4"x 3 1/4")**

**The cap pole is attached
with wood glue.
Cross bar is attached to
main pole with
counter-sunk flat head
screw. Base is attached
the same way.**

**Place Jesus on
dowel rods
attached to cross.**

Session 23

Session 23

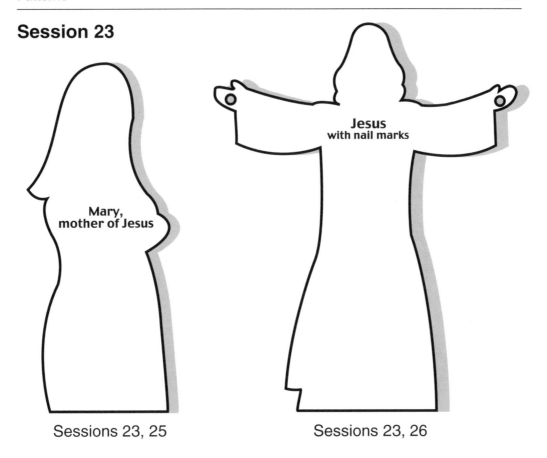

Sessions 23, 25   Sessions 23, 26

Jesus' tomb 18" x 9" x 7"

Tomb is constructed of newspaper balled up and taped together.
This shape is then covered with plaster cloth (available at any hobby
or craft shop), follow directions on package. After shape dries remove
newspaper and tape. Cut opening with jeweler's saw or keyhole
saw. Make separate "stone" for tomb. The dried version then can
be painted grays using a sponge technique to achieve
a stone appearance.

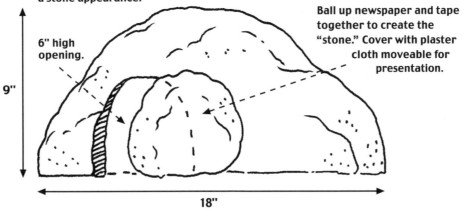

Sessions 23, 24

Session 24

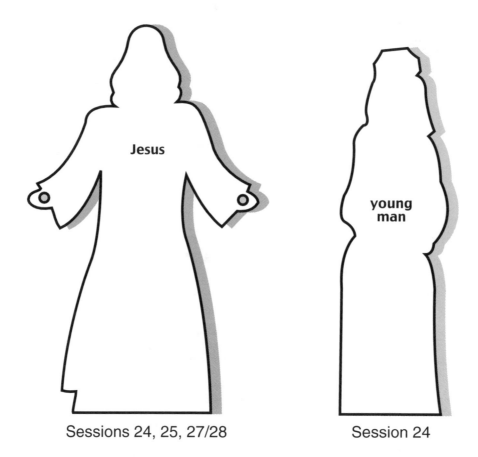

Sessions 24, 25, 27/28   Session 24

Session 25

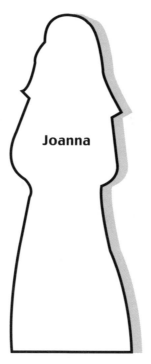

Joanna

Session 25

Top view of Thomas's table (8 1/2"x 3")

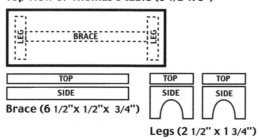

LEG   BRACE   LEG

TOP
SIDE

Brace (6 1/2"x 1/2"x 3/4")

TOP	TOP
SIDE	SIDE

Legs (2 1/2" x 1 3/4")

Session 25

**Attach 2" hinge on backside of each door
to allow door to open out of room.**

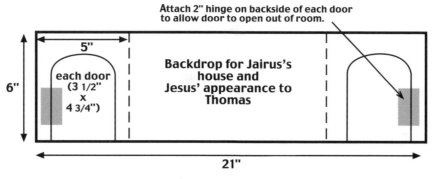

5"

6"

each door
(3 1/2"
x
4 3/4")

**Backdrop for Jairus's
house and
Jesus' appearance to
Thomas**

21"

Session 25

Session 26

The Great Commission

"All authority in heaven and on earth has been given to me. Go therefore and make disciples of all nations, baptizing them in the name

*of the Father and
of the Son and
of the Holy Spirit,*

*and teaching them to obey everything that
I have commanded you.*

*And remember,
I am with you always, to the end of the age."*

Matthew 28:18–20

Session 26

Session 27

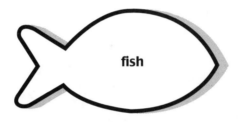

Sessions 27/28

Session 29

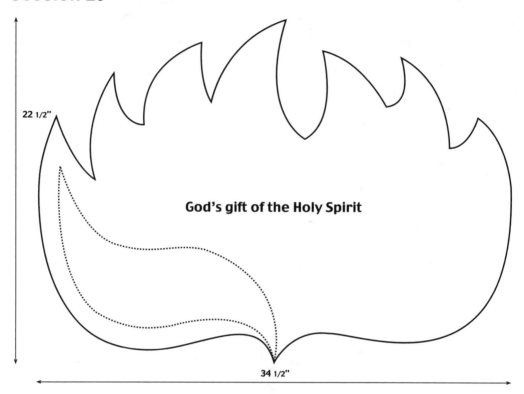

God's gift of the Holy Spirit

22 1/2"

34 1/2"

Session 29

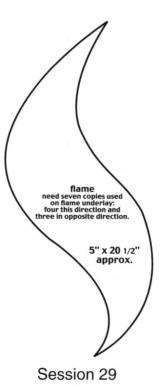

flame
need seven copies used
on flame underlay:
four this direction and
three in opposite direction.

**5" x 20 1/2"
approx.**

Session 29

Session 29

Spirit of Wisdom

Spirit of Understanding

Spirit of Counsel

Spirit of Might

Spirit of Knowledge

Session 29

Session 29

Spirit of Awe of God

Spirit of Joy in the Presence of God

Session 29

Session 30

lame man
with Peter

Session 30

Session 31

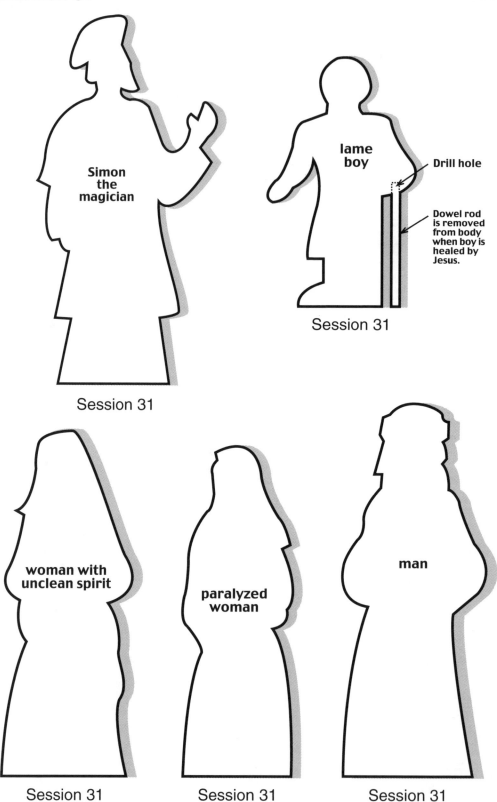

Simon the magician

Session 31

lame boy

Drill hole

Dowel rod is removed from body when boy is healed by Jesus.

Session 31

woman with unclean spirit

paralyzed woman

man

Session 31

Session 31

Session 31

Session 31

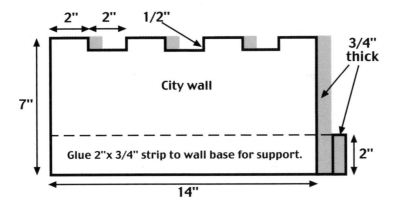

Session 31

Session 32

Dorcas

widow

Session 32

Session 32

Session 32

Session 32

Session 32

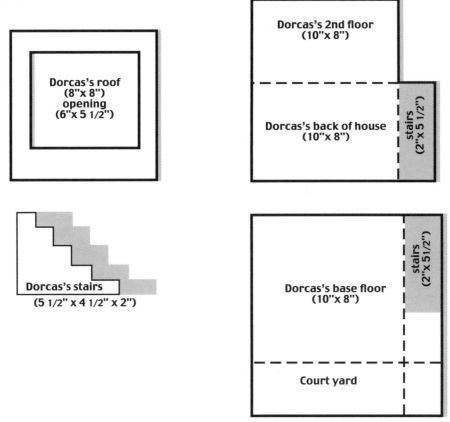

Dorcas's roof
(8"x 8")
opening
(6"x 5 1/2")

Dorcas's 2nd floor
(10"x 8")

Dorcas's back of house
(10"x 8")

stairs
(2"x 5 1/2")

Dorcas's stairs
(5 1/2" x 4 1/2" x 2")

Dorcas's base floor
(10"x 8")

stairs
(2"x 51/2")

Court yard

Session 32

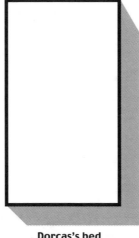

Dorcas's bed
(4 1/2" x 2 1/2" x 1 3/4")

Session 32

Session 33

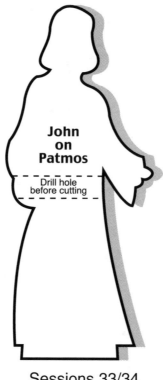

John
on
Patmos

Drill hole
before cutting

Sessions 33/34

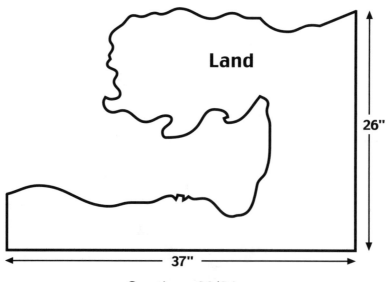

Land

26"

37"

Sessions 33/34

Session 33

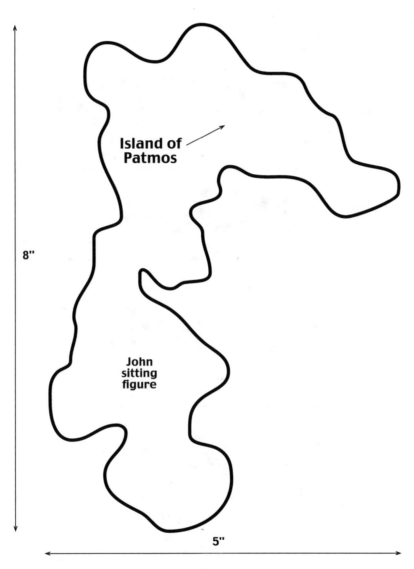

Sessions 33/34

Session 33

Jerusalem

Judea

Samaria

Ephesus

Sessions 33/34

Session 33

" I saw a new heaven and a new earth. And I saw the new Jerusalem, coming down out of heaven from God, and I heard a loud voice from the throne saying,
'Behold, the dwelling of God is with people.
God will live with them, and they shall be God's people. God will wipe away every tear from their eyes, there shall be no death, there shall be no sadness, or crying, or pain anymore. The old way is gone. God is making everything new' ".

Revelation 21:1–4

Session 34

" I saw a new heaven and a new earth. And I saw the holy city, the new Jerusalem. And I did not see the temple in the city, for the temple is God. And the city has no need of sun or moon to shine upon it, for the glory of God is its light,... By its light shall the nations walk; and the rulers of the earth will bring their glory into it, and its gates shall never be shut by day—and there shall be no night there; they need no light of lamp or sun, for God will be their light, and they shall reign for ever and ever."

Revelation 21: 22–26

Session 34